YOU MUST MONETIZE YOUR BOOK

CREATE MULTIPLE STREAMS OF INCOME,
DIVERSIFY YOUR EARNINGS,
AND MULTIPLY YOUR IMPACT

HONORÉE CORDER

AUTHOR, *YOU MUST WRITE A BOOK* &
YOU MUST MARKET YOUR BOOK

YOU MUST MONETIZE YOUR BOOK

CREATE MULTIPLE STREAMS OF INCOME, DIVERSIFY YOUR EARNINGS, AND MULTIPLY YOUR IMPACT

HONORÉE CORDER

AUTHOR, *YOU MUST WRITE A BOOK* & *YOU MUST MARKET YOUR BOOK*

ALSO BY HONORÉE CORDER

THE *YOU MUST* BOOK BUSINESS SERIES

- *You Must Write a Book: Boost Your Brand, Get More Business, and Become the Go-To Expert* & *I Must Write My Book: The Companion Workbook to You Must Write a Book*
- *You Must Market Your Book: Increase Your Impact, Sell More Books, and Make More Money* & *I Must Market My Book: The Companion Workbook to You Must Market Your Book*

OTHER WRITING BOOKS

- *There is No Such Thing as Writer's Block: You Can Unlock Your Inner Prolific Writer*
- *The Bestselling Book Formula: Write a Book that Will Make You a Fortune* & *The Bestselling Book Formula Journal*
- The *Like a Boss Book* Series
- *The Miracle Morning for Writers* with Hal Elrod & Steve Scott
- *The Prosperity for Writers* Book Series
- *Write Your First Nonfiction Book: A Primer for Aspiring Authors*

OTHER BOOKS & SERIES

- *Business Dating: Applying Relationship Rules in Business for Ultimate Success*
- *Stop Trying So F*cking Hard: Live Authentically, Design a Life You Love, and Be Happy (Finally)*
- *Tall Order: Organize Your Life and Double Your Success in Half the Time*
- *Vision to Reality: How Short Term Massive Action Equals Long Term Maximum Results*
- *The Divorced Phoenix: Rising from the Ashes of a Broken Marriage*
- *If Divorce is a Game, These are the Rules: 8 Rules for Thriving Before, During and After Divorce*
- *The Miracle Morning* Book Series with Hal Elrod
- *The Successful Single Mom* Book Series

Copyright 2024 © Honorée Enterprises Publishing, LLC

All rights reserved. No part of this book may be reproduced or transmitted in any form or by any means, electronic or mechanical, including photocopying, recording, or by any information storage and retrieval system without written permission of the publisher, except for the inclusion of brief quotations in a review.

Designed by Dino Marino, www.dinomarinodesign.com

Paperback ISBN: 978-1-947665-34-7

Hardcover ISBN: 978-1-947665-35-4

Digital ISBN: 978-1-947665-37-8

TABLE OF CONTENTS

INTRODUCTION I

SECTION I
LAYING THE FOUNDATION 1

CHAPTER ONE
Why Monetizing Your Book is the Next Best Thing You Can Do for Yourself and Your Business 3

CHAPTER TWO
Before You Monetize 7

CHAPTER THREE
Income Stream Considerations and Overview 14

CHAPTER FOUR
Income Stream Basics 18

SECTION II
INCOME STREAMS 25

CHAPTER FIVE
Coaching 27

CHAPTER SIX
Courses 32

CHAPTER SEVEN
Certifications 36

CHAPTER EIGHT
Consulting 42

CHAPTER NINE
Speaking 46

CHAPTER TEN
Training 53

CHAPTER ELEVEN
Turn Your Book into a Book Series 61

CHAPTER TWELVE
Selling Books in Bulk and Custom Printing 67

CHAPTER THIRTEEN
Virtual Summits 77

CHAPTER FOURTEEN
Mastering Your Mastermind 82

SECTION III
MONEY IN MOTION 87

CHAPTER FIFTEEN
Choosing Your Best and Fastest Path to Revenue 89

CONCLUSION
Insights, Final Thoughts, and Best Wishes 98

AUTHOR'S NOTES 106

GRATITUDE 108

COURSES 109

WHO IS HONORÉE CORDER? 111

SPECIAL INVITATION

Be sure to sign up for instant access to all of the resources and bonuses included in this book:

HonoreeCorder.com/Monetize

INTRODUCTION

Dear Reader,

This book is a long time coming and over twenty years in the making.

When I was a kid, my dad told me, "If you're working for *someone* else, that someone will get rich (and you probably won't)!" Or something to that effect. Hey, I was a kid, so I'm paraphrasing this quote. Is that even a thing? LOL

Anyway.

He encouraged me to work for myself so I'd have time and financial freedom. That advice has played over and over in my mind all these years, and it was the cause of me monetizing my books and building the empire I enjoy and am still building today.

It's important to point out that I was a foster kid and never made it to college. The odds weren't exactly stacked in my favor. But I was determined to find a way to work for myself and, despite any glaring limitations, achieve financial independence.

So, early in my twenties, I started my first business. Within minutes (okay, maybe days), I was *hooked*.

For context, I was in my twenties in the 1990s, before cell phones. The internet wasn't available to Jane Q. Citizen yet, and I didn't yet have email, a home computer, or a fax machine.

My first business was in network marketing. I sold health and wellness products (kinda still do, but not as a focus) for a company I had grown up with that happened to have a business opportunity built right in.

I didn't know what I didn't know (how to run a business, sales, selling, personal growth and development, leadership and developing leaders, and so much more). But I did know I wanted *freedom*, and more to the point, *financial freedom*. I also loved the products and knew they could help people. The business opportunity, plus the quality of the products, seemed to provide the perfect opportunity for me.

What I lacked in hard skills, I made up for with enthusiasm. My mentor, who was old enough to be my grandfather, told me, "If you set yourself on fire, people will come for miles around to watch you burn!"

First lesson: Enthusiasm is a little thing that makes a huge difference!

While I was running all over New York City, sharing my products, my upline mentor and his wife were doing all the packing and shipping. That was in the days of having an inventory, and my extra-tiny apartment didn't allow for any of that. I immediately dove into the personal development aspect of growing my business. The leaders in my company shared their collective tips about growing their business and how it always started with Person Zero. In this case, Person Zero was me.

I loved listening to the company's monthly motivational tapes. They included a product overview and interviews with company leadership. Those conversations were with distributors who were growing their businesses fast and making an impact on people's health, plus insight on creating an income that replaced their full-time professions. I couldn't get enough.

Count me in, I thought.

Enter: Anthony Robbins' book, *Awaken the Giant Within*. A friend recommended the book right about the time I started my business. Coincidentally, a few weeks later, I found myself at Tony's Unleash the Power Within seminar, which included *The Firewalk Experience*. (Yes, I did the fire walk. It was awesome. I've done it several more times. No, I didn't burn my feet. But I did light a fire within myself! (Highly recommend.)

Talk about a life, business, and game-changer.

Starting my business, combined with a focus on personal development, set me on a path I still traverse to this day.

It wasn't long before I was able to quit my job and replace my income. *And I wanted more.*

Once I'd proven to myself I could achieve just about anything I set my mind to, I started to look for other ways to earn income.

Through a series of synchronistic events, I found myself disenchanted with the company I was working with. They kept changing the compensation plan and didn't provide the progressive marketing and distribution opportunities some of the other similar (and, in my opinion, inferior) companies did. And eventually, I decided to focus outside of the industry.

During a fortuitous conversation with my business coach, I uncovered what would come next: business coaching.

With her help, my coaching business got off to a solid start. She helped me develop a marketing plan right away.

How do you market your coaching business? One way is by doing free speaking engagements. If you're good, eventually, someone will offer to pay.

I was a couple of years into coaching and speaking when I found myself a single mom, living in a new city. That's when I added corporate training to my menu of services. And on it went. *And that was before I wrote my first book.*

With my hindsight as your foresight, you'll be able to use your book as the basis for identifying, launching, and earning income from the contents of your book, combined with your expertise, education, and experience.

I'll share more about my story within the pages of this book, with insight and information about how you can repurpose your book into income stream after income stream.

You've got a book, but a book can be just the beginning! You can repurpose the contents into one, two, or dozens of other streams of income.

Each one can be *easy, lucrative, fast,* and *fun*!

Every year, I play The Money Game: New Income Stream Edition. What is it? Well, first, it's not a real game, so don't go to Amazon and do a search. It's my own personal game where I seek to identify what new six or seven-figure income stream (or two) I can develop that year. As of this writing, I've developed more than a dozen, and I have many, many more ideas in the queue.

You can play The Money Game, too, and you can *win*. This book is designed to help you play to win in the shortest and best way possible.

Some income streams I've kept (hello, books and courses!) and others I've let go (it was wonderful while it lasted, executive coaching and corporate training!). This book has my recipe for each income stream, and in the book bonuses (which you'll find at HonoreeCorder.com/Monetize), you'll find a few tools and resources to accelerate your journey.

Are you getting excited yet? I sure am! So here's what you can expect in this book.

It is divided into three sections:

SECTION I: LAYING THE FOUNDATION

In this first section, I help you get your ducks in a row and set the stage for choosing which income stream to develop first.

Yes, I know you might want "all of them." Me, too—believe me, I get it! Part of the reason I've developed so many is because I get bored easily. Once I conquer something, I'm ready for the next thing. Plus, some income streams have continued to pay me and require little or no time. This has left me with time to focus on my other "problem:" unending ideas!

Once you get in the flow of ideas, you'll find you have more ideas than time. (Note: grab a notebook, the *You Must Monetize Your Book Workbook*, or open the Notes app on your phone, name it *Ideas*, and keep track of those suckers.) Also, if money is your driver, at some point it won't be a concern because you'll have enough—then more than enough. And you just might turn growing and giving it into a game, too.

Once you've got your bearings and have determined what *type* of income stream(s) you'd like to build, we'll head into:

SECTION II: INCOME STREAMS

Section II is simple: I cover the income streams I've developed over the past twenty years and share how you can start implementing them in your business.

Each chapter covers an income stream and, where applicable, the different ways to implement it in your business.

For example, coaching is an income stream. There are dozens of different types of coaching (such as *life, business, and executive*) and several ways to deliver coaching (one-on-one, in a group, or at the corporate level).

I've done most of them in my years of experience, and I'll provide insight and information so you can make an intelligent choice for yourself and your business.

Because I know you'll be excited to move forward once you've discovered just the right income stream, I'll share my thoughts on how long it could take to realize revenue.

Each income stream requires a different amount of time before you can expect to earn any income. A quality book could take upward of a year or more; a course could start earning you money as soon as *tomorrow*.

A word of caution here: Your level of urgency around how fast you *need* to make money can color which income stream you choose. I'll talk more about this later, but it deserves a mention here that this can be counter-productive if *urgency* is the only filter you run a potential income stream through. You'll want to pay close and careful attention to the *other* considerations when choosing which income stream to stand up first. For now, remember this phrase:

SCARED MONEY DON'T MAKE MONEY.

There are more than a dozen possible income streams you can add to your empire included in this book. Several of them could work for you, but here's the best news of all: Even if none of them are the perfect fit, reading this book will prime your pump of ideas.

As I mentioned, you need a place to capture your ideas. And another word of warning: *they will flow*. Like water from a firehose, once they start to come, they will come fast and often. They'll pop into your mind even in the midst of working on something else. Stay focused, enjoy the idea flow, and simply capture them right away. Then, when it's time to decide what to do next, you'll have ideas to analyze.

More on this later—I just want to plant the seed that *this*, the monetization part of your book's life, is quite possibly the most fun and fulfilling of all. Lest you think I am all about the money, that is simply how I keep score. A lot of *income* can only mean one thing: there's a large chance I'm making a lot of *impact*.

SECTION III: MONEY IN MOTION

Section III is where we bring it all together. You've read through the different streams and possibly decided what *type* of income stream you want. Once you've identified the *actual* income stream that you want to launch first, it's time to get down to business. Let's get some money in motion right into your bank account.

Here's a wonderful thought: Your bank account can hold an unlimited amount! This Section is all about putting what you've learned and have committed to the test. You'll analyze your ideas, solidify which income stream to build, set a goal and craft a plan, take action, and begin to see money in motion.

Is it that simple? Yes, actually, it is.

There's much, much more on that to come.

Let's dive into it!

SECTION I
LAYING THE FOUNDATION

CHAPTER ONE

WHY MONETIZING YOUR BOOK IS THE NEXT BEST THING YOU CAN DO FOR YOURSELF AND YOUR BUSINESS

You wrote a book, and that is awesome! *Congratulations!*

Before we dive into what *else* you can do with your book, let's take a moment and reflect on the magic that is being an author.

When Mark Victor Hansen told me, "*You must write a book!*" I had no idea just how much that statement would change my life. But this isn't my reflection time. It's yours.

Take a deep breath and think about the people you've met. The clients you've attracted to your business. The places you've gone. If your experience is anything like mine and the hundreds of authors I've worked with, this is an incredibly fun exercise.

All because you wrote your book.

Wow! Right?

Reflecting on everything that's happened can provide a peek into what can happen when you decide to monetize it—i.e., repurpose your book's contents. It can also help you decide *how* to monetize them.

Deciding to use your book as the basis for a coaching program, expanding it into an online course, keynote presentation, or any one of more than a dozen income streams will increase your income *and* your impact.

A book is a wonderful thing (and income stream), but a book is just a jumping-off point.

I can almost hear some haters who cannot wait to post their one-star review: "She's all about the money!" So let me talk to y'all first. Because if that's your initial reaction, and because this is my book, I get to say, *you need to get your money mindset in order.* I mean this in the most loving way possible.

If what I'm saying doesn't resonate with you, please return the book and get a refund.

If you know you have some work to do on your prosperity consciousness, I have a book on money mindset that will help, *Prosperity for Writers.* If you're open to expanding your thoughts on money (so you can make more of it easier), that would be a great read for you. To save you some time, allow me to help you regardless of whether you want to set me on fire because you think I'm a money grubber, or you're truly open to some effective ideas:

- **People who make a lot of money are mostly good.** In fact, *we* are the ones who pay for everything. I pay taxes (a lot of them) and support organizations that help others. Even a percentage of what you spent on this book will support my philanthropic endeavors.
- **You need to play bigger, because playing small doesn't serve you or the world.** If you've got a message that could help others, you must get that message in the hands, minds, and hearts of as many people as possible.
- **You can make as much as you can believe you can make.** The sky is the limit, and your bank account can handle as

much as you want to put in it. There are customers at every price point, and when you provide enough value, people will happily pay whatever you charge. (And, if, right out of the gate, you think something is "too expensive," it might be time to focus on expanding your income rather than on your limited budget.)

If you saw the word *monetize* and it made you angry because you think focusing on making a bigger income isn't a great idea, please explain to me how that helps you or anyone else. You can't because you making less of an income—*and an impact*—doesn't serve anyone. Not you, not your potential clients or customers, and certainly not the greater good.

Why not, instead, focus on how you can serve others, and as a result, you will do well from doing good. And for the purposes of this book, I'm going to assume you're excited to see all of the magic that can happen when you monetize your book.

MONETIZING FOR IMPACT AND INCOME

I wasn't kidding when I said having a book is a wonderful thing. But having a book can be just the start of what you can do with your unique combination of experience, education, knowledge, connections, and more. Yes, to create an income and an impact.

You might know about some or even all of the options, but for those just tuning into the station of My Book Makes Money (MBMM-FM), here are two you might not have considered:

- **Coloring books.** Adult coloring books are the fastest-growing segment of print publishing. They are all the rage among executives stuck in Zoom meeting after Zoom meeting. Therapists suggest adults use them to help with anxiety and quiet their minds as a form of meditation. Creating a coloring book with your message in the images can expand your footprint as an author while simultaneously helping people who really need it.

- **Training.** Corporate training can command upwards of $25,000 *per day*. Develop your book into a training manual, and you'll get to work with and directly serve folks who are ready to embrace your message at a deeper level.

Your book might be doing its job. You're earning royalty income and booking speaking gigs or engaging new coaching clients.

Yet some of my most fun conversations with authors center around creating additional income streams.

You mean I can turn my book into a series? Yes.

It's possible to get and charge more for speaking engagements? Yes.

I can create live and online courses and earn additional income? Yes.

All of the above and more.

Most authors I know are not satisfied with the amount of money they earn from their books.

I'm here to help you see a future where your income is diversified. One with multiple income streams coming together to create financial stability and certainty. One that allows creativity and flexibility. Most of all, one that allows for total freedom.

Monetizing to me means continuously creating additional streams of income, and allowing for time and financial freedom.

Because I *think* you picked up this book because that's what you want to do, I say we should go ahead and get into it! There is much to consider when deciding which income stream(s) to tackle first. Come with me into Chapter Two and allow me to help you gain some clarity.

CHAPTER TWO

BEFORE YOU MONETIZE

The first time I heard the phrase *repurpose content*, I was intrigued. I didn't know for sure what it was or how to do it, but intuitively, I knew it warranted an investigation.

I was in a workshop at a conference, and the speaker talked about how a book's content could be a workbook, keynote speech, or even the basis for a conference. Mind blown.

Okay, I wonder if I can do this, I thought.

I took the contents of my first book, *Tall Order! Organize Your Life and Double Your Success in Half the Time* (I know— not my best title, but it's a crowd-pleaser—you might like it), and repurposed the content into the Rainmaker Bootcamp. Within a few days of creating the workshop's outline and the manual to go with it, I pitched it to a dear friend who was a partner at a law firm.

She'd previously confided that her "babies" (young associates) were far less productive than they could be and were not developing business as they should be. She loved the idea of the workshop, got it approved, and less than a month later, I had a signed contract, fifty percent down on a $5,000 day of training, and was marketing it to other law firms.

This workshop became a steady income earner in my business, and it checked several important professional boxes for me:

- It was *easy* for me to teach. I knew the content well, the participants enjoyed learning the material, and it helped them.
- It was *lucrative*. I was paid well for one day of training.
- It was *fun*. I loved helping professionals learn how to generate more business, which helped them further their careers.
- Eventually, I combined this workshop training with coaching—and sold them as a package.

Additionally, it checked a couple of personal boxes for me as well:

- It allowed me to spend most of my time at home. As a single mom, my goal was to travel as little as possible.
- As an introvert, I hoped to leave home as little as possible. Smile.

I'll circle back to this again later, but before you decide which income stream to develop, you'll want to determine a few things (just keep them in mind for now):

- How *fast* do you need revenue? You will want to pick a stream that matches your urgency to earn money.
- How *easy, lucrative, and fun* (ELF) do you want it to be? You probably don't want to just earn money; you might want to earn money in an easy way, that is lucrative, and also fun. Developing a new income stream doesn't have to be hard. And you might as well enjoy the journey, right?
- How involved do you want to be? Do you mind trading time for money, or would you prefer to develop streams that pay you forever with little to no involvement once

they are in place? Or do you want both?

I *loved* coaching, and as you'll see, I delivered it in several different ways. It was easy and lucrative. *However*, all of them required my time. That is, until I figured out a way to create a course based on my material.

My goal was, and almost always is, to figure out how to leverage my income streams. I take the time to build them, launch and then nurture them, and then allow them to continue to pay me while I do something else.

FREEDOM, FINANCES, OR FAME?

When monetizing your book, in addition to ELF, there are three Fs to consider. Really, this applies to building your business and, ultimately, your empire.

I want a business and empire I own, not one that owns me. I don't want to *have* to do anything. Therefore, one of my highest values is freedom. Of the three, freedom, finances, and fame, freedom is number one by a landslide. Even greater than any desire I have for money, I value freedom. Fame ranks a distant third.

You get to decide which order you rank them in:

1. Freedom
2. Finances
3. Fame

Or:

1. Finances
2. Freedom
3. Fame

I'll caution you against putting fame first (or even second). I've seen many people sacrifice their freedom and finances for fame. While they have a lot of name and face recognition, they still struggle financially, and certainly don't have a ton of freedom.

I've built my business around having time and money freedom by intentionally building income streams that don't require a lot of time once I've put them in place—primarily books and courses, but also partnerships, certifications, referral and affiliate opportunities, and more. I've shared them all in this book, with insight and information (as well as processes, procedures, and cautions) so you can decide which ones might work best for you.

You may need to rank finances higher than freedom for a period of time, with the goal of switching them at some point. I've also seen my peers sacrifice their freedom for a buck or two, only to realize they didn't get the outcome they truly wanted.

I mention this here because once you start to see some of the possibilities, you might want to do them all. I get it. Building income streams is kinda the best. You'll avoid unnecessary pain and suffering when you've got clarity *before* you choose.

Before you read any further, rank your Fs. Their order will help you decide which stream fits the best.

Then, as you're looking at each stream, ask yourself, is it as ELF as I want or need it to be? Keep this in mind as you read through Chapter Three and the remainder of the book.

Speaking of Chapter Three, it is an overview of possible income streams. Before we can really dive into "which income stream to build," we need to make one more stop first and discuss . . .

BUILDING THE BUSINESS (AND EMPIRE) YOU TRULY WANT

Have you ever heard the expression: I've been climbing the ladder and making really great time, only to realize it was leaning against the wrong wall?

I see this a lot, especially when building a business, and even more so when it comes to authors writing books. I'm an entrepreneur, but many of my close friends are not. Most of the people I serve the community with are not. And, most of the people I meet at networking events are not. Suffice it to say I can count on one hand the number of highly paid professionals I meet who are completely in love with what they do for money. They might make a really great living, but they don't seem to be living a really great life.

But lest you think all of my full-time entrepreneurial friends are blissed out, you would be mistaken. Some of them traded forty or fifty-hour weeks working for someone else (while not being particularly happy) to work more than fifty hours for themselves and are equally, if not more, unhappy.

Wait, what?

Yes, it's true—they jumped from one less-than-ideal situation to another. The grass isn't always greener, *unless* you take some time to gain clarity. Your formula for success, even as you're shopping for a new income stream, or several, is: *Look*, then *choose*, then *move*. Let me explain.

I hear an awful lot of "That sounds good! I'll do that!" when it comes to income stream creation and even book writing.

Someone will decide they want to be a coach, get certified through the International Coach Federation (ICF), and then they're a coach. They've gone through that effort without considering the amount of time it takes to build a coaching business—without realizing the amount of time and energy coaching, one-on-one, will take *once they've engaged the client*.

A business built with the idea of freedom in mind is not necessarily a business that should be built around providing services (unless you can charge very high fees).

The same thing happens with books. Almost every day, I talk to an aspiring author who has an idea for a book but doesn't take the time to analyze the true marketability of the book, the market size, or whether the book will help them achieve what they want.

Look

Look is the directive for taking the time to see an income stream for what it is, and what it isn't. Looking at potential streams is like shopping—you determine what's available and analyze the investment.

Choose

Once you've figured out what's available, based on your criteria, you choose the one that fits.

If you just write and publish a book without strategy or forethought, especially if you professionally publish it, you may invest in something with a low or no likelihood of return.

If you launch an income stream without strategy or forethought, no one will buy it, and you'll be tempted to think it is a reflection of *you* when, in fact, it is a reflection of your lack of strategy and forethought.

Choose the income stream that is in alignment with the empire you want to build and based on the life you want to live.

Move

Then, and only then, will you *move*. In other words, you won't take action on an income stream until you're confident it fits into the big picture—*your* big picture.

You want an income stream you will enjoy building, love selling, and benefit from having around.

Until you are able to just try on an income stream for the heck of it (like I did when I founded the Empire Builders Mastermind, which I talk about in Chapter Fourteen), please spend extra time analyzing and applying strategy before you *move*.

I would be remiss if I didn't tell you that you might need to slow down to speed up. I see many folks who are busy, but they aren't accomplishing much; they aren't moving the needle. Or they're very busy doing, but what they're doing isn't moving the right needle. They won't get where they think they want to go, and that's a bummer. I don't want that to happen to you, okay? Okay!

Now that I've helped you avoid becoming a cautionary tale (you're welcome), you can start to *look*. I've got some other considerations for you in the next chapter.

When you're ready, join me there.

CHAPTER THREE

INCOME STREAM CONSIDERATIONS AND OVERVIEW

I'm looking forward to hearing about the magic that happens as a result of you reading this chapter—and the rest of this book.

BEFORE YOU CHOOSE AN INCOME STREAM...

When you're looking through the options, here are some questions to answer *before* you choose a revenue stream:

- **How soon do I need revenue?** Without question, writing a book (a quality book that will be a best earner) can take the longest to monetize. The first question to ask when it's time to monetize your book is, *How soon do I need revenue?* Followed by, *How much do I need to earn?*

- **How much time do I have to build my income stream?** If you're pressed for time because you have personal responsibilities or even a full-time job, you'll need to have a real conversation about how much time you can devote to the building phase.

- **How much money do I have to invest?** Some income streams require more of an initial investment than others. While I do love a shoestring budget, I recognize my outcomes are borne by my willingness to do things professionally and well, from the beginning. Be honest about how much you're willing to invest in relation to your expectations on the other side.

- **Who can help me avoid painful mistakes and gain momentum faster?** You won't be reinventing any wheels here, which means there are many resources available to help you gain success and avoid failure. Consider engaging a mentor or coach, or joining a mastermind. Riding the entrepreneur rollercoaster can be a lonely ride, so buckle up with some peer and mentor support.

- **How can I build a new income stream and thoroughly enjoy the process?** I'll answer this one for you—in addition to the above, setting the right expectations for yourself can be helpful. I've sprinkled more advice on this throughout the book, but the first thing is to remember why you're starting in the first place. You want time or money freedom, to build something you enjoy that helps others—these or even something else. You *can* do this, and you *can* definitely enjoy the process! Do your best, give yourself grace when life happens, and lean on your mentor, coach, and fellow entrepreneurs when you need to!

THE INCOME STREAMS

Okay—now, I'm sure you're ready to get down to the business of identifying your next income stream. It has taken us a bit to get here. You know this is because I want you to succeed, right? I hope so.

Each income stream has a unique combination of possibilities and opportunities, and for each one, I'll share the framework that will help you design the one you choose so it fits you. No sense in building an income stream, only to realize you don't love it. If you wanted to do that, you'd just go get a *job*. Amiright?

I've compiled my experience (hindsight being 20/20 and all that) and my observations in working with authorpreneurs and empire builders to share what you need to know to truly be successful with whatever stream speaks to you.

Because, hopefully, you've pre-determined your Fs and your ELF needs, you should be able to identify which income stream(s) would likely be the best fit. Then, after you read Chapter Four, you can just jump to the chapter where I provide your road map for putting your chosen income stream in place.

Note: I recommend choosing one, *maaaaaybe* two, new income streams to launch per year.

I know, you're going to want to do them all (me, too), but solid, recurring, successful income streams take time to nurture and mature.

Yes, I've developed a lot of income streams. I identified, planned, launched, and enjoyed working on them—mostly one at a time!

You will note that there are a few instances where "batching" (launching two) income streams is possible. For example, launching a book and a companion book, such as a planner or journal, is a fantastic way to put two products into the market at the same time.

Launching a book and a course, based on the same content, can also be a successful one-two punch. The course, based on the contents of your book, could even come *before* your book. You'll find a link to a video I did about my book *plus* companion book *plus* course strategy called the Three-Legged Stool in the book resources at HonoreeCorder.com/Monetize.

However, I encourage you to think through either of those and have a clear plan with an abundance of time built into your creation period and launch strategy.

As I share my experience with each income stream, I hope one will either fit like a glove, inspire you to customize it, or create a new one that does!

Here are some of the income stream options I've shared in this book:

- Coaching
- Courses
- Certifications
- Consulting
- Speaking
- Training
- Turn your book into a series
- Selling books in bulk
- Custom books
- Virtual summits
- Masterminds

To build an income stream to its potential, you must know how to lay the foundation for its success. While each one is different in strategy and execution, they all have several things in common. I know you want to know what they are, so please keep reading.

CHAPTER FOUR

INCOME STREAM BASICS

You're probably very excited to get started building your new income streams. I feel you on this one. I feel a rush of excitement every time I have a new idea, it seems solid, *and* it passes muster. But hold your horses, empire builder! I want you to flourish, not fail.

Some necessary and very un-exciting pre-work is needed to ensure any enterprise you embark on flies. Whether you're launching an entirely new business or simply an income stream, there are some basic boxes you'll need to check so all you do is win, win, win, no matter what, what, what!

PRODUCT + PRICE + BUYER + STRUCTURE + MARKETING + PLAN = SUCCESS!

These criteria—a product, price, buyer, structure, marketing, and plan—are the basis for your income stream—regardless of what it is.

Product. Every income stream is a program (coaching or speaking, perhaps) or process (consulting or certification). It has its own blend of special procedures and delivery, the ingredients that differentiate it from the other income streams.

And:

Price. How much are you charging? *What are you or your product or service worth?*

Add:

Buyer. You must have a customer or a client. If there are no buyers, there is no income.

Plus:

Structure. There's a structure that wraps around your ability to deliver your product or service.

Then:

Marketing. Connect what you're selling to probable purchasers; that's marketing in a nutshell. Plan to spend the lion's share of your time, at least initially, on marketing.

Finally:

Plan. You must have a plan to bring it all into being. Fail to plan, and you plan to fail. But you're going to plan to succeed, and you will!

THE PRODUCT: WHAT ARE YOU SELLING?

Obviously, you need to decide which income stream you want to build. If you've already done this, fantastic! If you haven't yet, go ahead and read this entire chapter and perhaps skim over the income streams. You'll either find an income stream that will be *just right,* or you'll be inspired to design something entirely new.

If you're thinking, *That's what I got this book for, Honorée. I want to build something with your guidance. Duh!* I understand. I'd love for you to take something I've done and be able to "plug and play," and if that works out, fantastic! If not, I encourage you to think about how you could use the fundamentals of building an income stream plus your potential to take a piece of one and apply it to another. Thus, you'd be creating something completely unique to you, your needs, and the business you want to build.

THE PRICE: HOW MUCH?

This could be a chapter—or even a book—on its own. In fact, I recommend you read *Value-Based Fees* by Alan Weiss as your primer for success in pricing.

If you're a beginner, charge beginner prices, but only for a while and only as long as you're testing the market. Once upon a time, I charged $15,000 for something I now command $100,000 for. I quickly learned the return on investment for my clients was hundreds of thousands, and for some, into the millions of dollars. My fee is a rounding error. Is it a large sum of money? Yes and no.

You must charge what you and your service or product are worth and not a penny less. Do your research. Analyze your results and the results of your past clients. Determine your price and speak it with confidence.

If you have more of a commodity item, use common sense and add in whatever you need to do to differentiate yourself from the market.

The end of this chapter has a section on sales and selling. Read it at least three times, unless you have one hundred percent confidence in your ability, your product, and your price (then read it twice).

THE BUYER: WHO IS IT?

Each income stream has a buyer—your client or customer. I call them my *avatar*, or ideal buyer. The very next step after identifying an income stream is to clarify who it is designed to help. *In detail.*

My avatar for this book (you!) is the person who has a nonfiction book, probably prescriptive or transformative nonfiction, and wants to repurpose the contents into different income streams.

There are other details, but in a nutshell, you are who I had in mind as I sat and wrote this book each morning.

Write a list of the qualities and characteristics of your avatar. Hint: they are exactly the same as the ideal reader of your book if you're basing your new income stream on the same content.

Include: *age range, gender, profession, personality traits*, problems you solve, etc.* My list has more than twenty-five bullet points, usually based on someone I've already worked with. I mean, have you ever worked with someone and loved every minute? (Me, too.) That person is who I have in mind when I'm creating my avatar profile.

*I include personality traits because, in a perfect world, you won't just read this book; we're going to connect in real life (IRL). I don't know about you, but I want to connect with positive, growth-minded people who are fun to work with. So, I include that in my description and set the intention that it's those people who will want to connect with me.

THE STRUCTURE: PRODUCT DELIVERY

Your structure is how you define the delivery of your product. For instance, delivering a keynote presentation will generally take forty-five minutes to an hour. If you are a coaching executive or small business owner, you need to consider whether you will deliver your coaching sessions once a week, twice a month, or something else.

If you're creating a companion product, such as a journal or workbook, will it be paperback or hardcover? Large or small? Hundreds of pages, more or less?

MARKETING: DEVELOPING BUSINESS FROM THE BEGINNING

You absolutely must have a solid marketing plan. Once you've identified the other aspects of your new income stream, you need to figure out how you will bring it to market. Every income stream is different, but they all have one thing in common: They must be talked about in one way or another (website, webinar, one-on-one conversations, through social media posts or advertising, etc.) to connect your goods to buyers.

THE PLAN: BRINGING IT TO LIFE

Every successful income stream starts with a solid plan. A vision without a plan is just a dream. You can envision a wildly successful income stream all day long; however, without a plan, a massive action plan, in fact, the chances of "wild success" diminish rapidly. Have a solid plan, however, and your chances of being successful *sooner* exponentially increase.

Your plan must include:

- Product
- Price
- Customer or client profile
- Delivery structure
- Marketing
- How much time it can take, reasonably, to realize revenue

A solid plan you execute with intention and perseverance will make the difference between your short and long-term success and failure.

PROCESSES AND PROCEDURES

Every income stream requires processes and procedures. Here's the very least of what you need to get started. You will, of course, add more bells and whistles as time goes on.

- **Website and Copy.** While none of the income streams require a storefront, you need a place for prospects to land—one stop that allows them to browse your wares and decide what works. A simple one-page website with an overview will get you started, and over time, you can expand it into what works best for your empire.
- **Agreement/Contract.** Once a prospect is ready to engage you, they must sign an agreement or contract. "Good fences make great neighbors." I often use this saying about signing a legal agreement instead of relying on a handshake. Having a solid agreement is important for *both* parties. You can even provide a link to yours right on your web page and require an acknowledgment and a signature. Alternatively, you can use a virtual service like DocuSign. In my course, **Building a Million Dollar Book Business** (the companion course for this book), you'll find multiple legal agreements you can use as templates or provide to your attorney to customize.
- **Deliverables.** You'll need a way to deliver that for which your client has paid. A link to your digital workbook or to schedule time on your calendar once they've paid—no matter what you're delivering, be sure to map out how it will be received most efficiently and effectively.

Bookmark this page and plan to come back here once you've decided on an income stream.

A FEW WORDS ABOUT STICKY SUBJECTS

Sales. Selling. Overcoming objections. Commanding a price. Scope creep. If you have issues with sales or selling, asking what you're worth, or setting boundaries with clients or customers, now is a great time to sort those things out.

This book doesn't help you to do any of those things, but they are, without question, fundamental to any success you could have.

In the book's bonuses/resources, I've curated a list of the books, resources, and people I recommend to help guide you to success in each area.

Because.

No income stream sells itself. You must be a confident salesperson.

If you are hesitant to set a price and hold the line, you will struggle. You must be confident in your pricing and not compromise or settle once you decide on your fee.

If "scope creep" (allowing clients to push the boundaries of your time, services, or both) is an issue, you will always do more than you're paid to do. *People will treat you the way you allow them to.* Nonnegotiable: Setting clear boundaries *via your Contract or Agreement* and how you handle client interactions is absolutely essential. More than twice, I've quoted my Agreement with a client who pushed the limits of what we had agreed upon. One hundred percent of the time, we were able to continue because we had put our commitment in writing.

ARE YOU READY?

Now that I've covered the preliminaries, let's dive into just a few of the unlimited income streams you can develop from your book. Let the fun begin!

SECTION II
INCOME STREAMS

CHAPTER FIVE

COACHING

Although I began with coaching as my first official income stream, it actually pre-dated my book. As I mentioned, I was coaching and speaking to promote my coaching business for several years prior to writing my first book.

Even if you've been coaching for decades, a book can provide a line of sight to new avenues of coaching. If you've written your book in anticipation of using it to generate new coaching clients, it can do that, too.

There are three different ways I delivered coaching, two of which were developed *after* I published my first book. I started, as most coaches do, with one-on-one coaching. Once I gained traction and realized I had a full practice, I decided to try group coaching. This eventually led to corporate coaching.

First, a breakdown of each type of coaching, then my suggestions for engaging each type of clientele.

TYPES OF COACHING

One-on-one coaching helps clients overcome challenges, achieve goals, and improve performance.

In essence, one-on-one coaching revolves around sharing experiences and knowledge about specific topics, helping clients identify and resolve issues, and creating plans structured to assist them in reaching a specific result.

With this kind of coaching, a coach is helping one client at a time, offering time and expertise in exchange for money, while focusing on a client's unique and specific needs.

One-on-one coaching often happens in the form of coaching sessions via telephone or even virtual meetings.

One-on-one coaching is perhaps the most popular and used coaching option. Utilizing this option, you're giving the most attention and energy to an individual client, and naturally, you can command a fee that is extremely profitable (albeit somewhat limited, as time is limited, and therefore, it is not scalable).

Group coaching has the same potential benefits as one-on-one coaching, but while each client gets less individual attention from a coach, they can benefit from the coaching the other group members receive.

I've worked in groups as small as five or six, and as large as twenty. I would guess a group of four would work just as well, as in larger groups, the coach must focus to ensure each member is being heard *from*, as well as gaining an effective amount of value.

The benefit of groups for coaches is *leverage*. Each client pays less for group coaching than one-on-one coaching, but the coach has an increased income per hour, sometimes by many multiples.

Corporate coaching can take the form of one-on-one or group coaching (or both within the same company). The company recognizes it needs outside help and expertise, and coaching has become a popular go-to resource. The outcomes and goals are the same, regardless of who is paying the bill: overcome challenges, achieve goals, and improve performance.

ENGAGEMENT

One-on-one coaching engagements are perhaps the easiest and quickest. While it has on occasion taken a year or more to engage one particular client, I've also met, had a conversation with, and had a signed agreement and payment from a new client on the same day, within a few hours. There's no red tape here—the client is the decision maker and, therefore, can decide as quickly as *right now*.

Group coaching engagements have a longer runway. First, you have to decide how many spots are available in your group and then have enough prospective client meetings to engage the right number of clients.

When I was facilitating the Short-Term Massive Action (STMA) 100-Day Group Coaching for women, it took me a couple of rounds with smaller groups to reach my goal of twenty participants. By the time I had done four rounds, I had expanded from one full group to two.

Corporate coaching engagements differ from individual and group coaching in that you're engaging one entity—one contract and one payment can be awesome! You'll work with one or maybe two folks within a company to put together a program that works with the needs, goals, and challenges of their employees.

Remember this: Developing this type of client takes the longest. My shortest engagement time was a few months; my longest was *seven years*. Yes, it took me seven years to close the deal (with monthly and quarterly follow-up), but it was an extremely lucrative multi-year engagement.

Obviously, if you are looking for the shortest path to an income, start with one-on-one coaching, but keep your eyes on the group and corporate options. They are well worth the time and effort it takes to develop them.

THE BUSINESS OF COACHING

There are a few items you need to have in order, and a few things to keep in mind when setting up a coaching business and working with individuals or corporations.

Have a Deliverable. Have something to accompany your coaching program, such as a manual or workbook, to send to your clients when they begin coaching. Having something tangible to go with something as sometimes nebulous as coaching can provide peace of mind to the client.

An Agreement. You'll not only need an Agreement, but you'll also need to have it *signed* prior to coaching (even if you provided a free or discovery session in advance). Be sure to have yours written by an attorney who understands your business.

Payment Processing. I suggest accepting all types of client payments to make it easy to pay you. Accept checks, credit cards, and even digital payments (such as Venmo). You can even use a credit card processor through your business bank.

How to Charge for Coaching

Coaching fees can range from $150 to $25,000 per hour or more. If you're a new coach, you'll probably want to start between $300 and $500 per session (I recommend fifty-minute sessions). If you've been coaching for a decade or more, and depending upon your specialty—and adding in the bump you get from being an author—you'll want to charge no less than $1,000 per session and more if you have special expertise.

Remember: You are not charging for your *time*. You are charging for the magical combination of being an author, plus your years of experience, education, training, and your "mileage." You're giving access to **all of that** to your client, and that can be a ton of value! **Charge accordingly, proudly, and with confidence.**

TIME TO REVENUE?

Building a full, robust, and lucrative coaching business can take years. However, you can define, announce, and start earning money from coaching within a few weeks.

CHAPTER SIX

COURSES

Courses are now one of my very favorite income streams! I'll share why, of course, but it didn't start that way.

I created a couple of courses; both were recorded audio only because that's what was "hot" at the time and also what I had the ability and desire to do.

Then, I stopped creating courses because I perceived them as too difficult to do well (probably how a lot of folks feel about books). A fortuitous meeting with an experienced course creator changed my life (and my bank account).

It's a longer story, but here it is in brief: I met someone who had created several courses, and one of his launches grossed almost $300,000 in a weekend. He convinced me I should create a course, and I went kicking and screaming into the venture. *I'm so glad I did!*

Here's why: Courses can be a lucrative way to turn the contents of your book into an additional income stream. In fact, they can make more income and impact *faster* than a book. You still *must* have a book for all of the reasons I've shared ad nauseam.

But a course, my friend, can boost your bottom line in an easy, lucrative, and fun way. You can create a landing page for your course with just an outline, share that landing page, and collect pre-orders in as little as a day.

Astounding, right? I thought so, too.

TIME TO REVENUE?

Courses can generate revenue almost immediately (especially if you allow a special group to test the course by creating a BETA version with a pre-sale landing page). In addition to being a short-term revenue source, they can boost your bottom line long-term.

I've done courses in three different ways:

- **Live.** The Prosperity for Writers Course, on which a book of the same name is based, was taught live. (I also recorded it almost a decade ago and still sell it. Four one-hour calls, recorded, with a bit of homework.) Publishing Ph.D. was originally a live-only course I taught via Zoom. You can teach a course live via a conference call line (although that would be considered "old school" these days) or on a virtual video platform like Zoom or Google Hangout.

- **Recorded.** My original courses were recorded in two ways: The Prosperity for Writers Course was first hosted and taught on a conference call line, recorded and shared with the attendees, and eventually bundled and sold as a course.

- **Blended Learning.** My pre-recorded and on-demand courses are now something called "blended learning" (see bullet below). This means they come with videos, downloadable tools, text, and audio. All three of my flagship courses (Publishing Ph.D., Book Marketing Mastery, and Building a Million Dollar Book Business, the latter is the companion to this book) encompass the blended learning model and include the live component of a monthly Q&A.

Once I discovered that a blended learning model was the most efficacious for my students, I adopted it because I always put myself in the learner's seat.

Ask yourself these two simple questions:

- If I were my student, learning my material, how could I best learn, retain, and use it?
- As a customer, how would I like to be treated?

My courses have made me several hundred thousand dollars in the years I've been selling them, and I promise you I have left money on the table. While they are one of my favorite business assets—fun to create, launch, and sell—I'm still learning the intricacies of producing great courses and getting better at marketing them.

For that reason, I want to introduce you to an expert. If this chapter has piqued your interest, I want to direct you to someone who has an abundance of knowledge, experience, and success to help you create your courses most effectively right from the start.

Just like publishing a book without a true understanding of how to optimize the process will mean less income and impact, the same goes for courses. What you don't know can hurt you as much as what you think you know.

Between recording my first several courses and today, I've met and created a partnership with course expert, Lucas Marino. He's a Thinkific expert, and that's his platform of choice. He has two successful training companies, Marino Training and East Partnership, and together we've created the Empire Builders MasterClass (EmpireBuildersMasterClass.com.) He's the person I lean on to guide me through course creation because he knows all of the tiny details I don't want to screw up.

He is to courses what I am to books.

I suggest you grab his books, *Monetize Your Book with a Course* and *Course Pricing Strategies*. Then, make a visit to his website, https://www.marinotraining.com. I can't recommend creating a course to accompany your book highly enough—I hope you do one for the experience alone!

CHAPTER SEVEN

CERTIFICATIONS

Certifications are one of my very favorite income streams. I've created three different certifications in my career to allow professionals to use my processes in their businesses.

The three I've developed are:

1. The Single Mom Transformation Program (SMTP) is based on *The Successful Single Mom* book, and the group I formed to write the book for divorce attorneys and Certified Divorce Financial Planners.

2. The Short-Term Massive Action (STMA) 100-Day Coaching Program for business and executive coaches.

3. The Divorce Transformation Coaching Program (DTCP) is for divorce coaches and mediators.

Certifications are typically designated credentials earned by an individual to verify their legitimacy and competency in a particular process. If you are a professional who has developed a popular and profitable process you use with clients, chances are other professionals would like to and could benefit from using it as well. If so, you might want to consider creating a certification program.

THE BENEFITS

First, the benefits for you: You'll have another stream of income (or more than one) if you charge for your certification or receive a percentage of the income received by the certified individual or both. In addition, you will leverage the number of people who can be helped by the process you've developed. While I could help *some* single moms by hosting the SMTP, I've helped far more by having certified facilitators hosting hundreds of groups around the world.

The benefits to those you certify are multi-faceted. Having a certification provides confidence that they know what they are doing and helps them stand out among their peers. It will increase their number of clients and, therefore, their income. It is a true win-win-win.

TIME TO REVENUE?

The time to revenue is two-fold: You must first create a process others can benefit from (which can take years). But if you already have a process, it could take just a few months to create your certification program.

CREATING YOUR CERTIFICATION PROGRAM

There are four main steps to creating your certification:

Step 1: Develop the Program Content

The first step is to develop the program content. *What is the goal of the certification? Who exactly is it for? What needs to be included so you can meet that goal and your students can as well?*

Once you know the program's goals and the scope of the content, you can begin developing it to include course materials, training structure, and determine who would benefit from the certification.

You will want to, as with every income stream, develop a solid avatar profile: profession, their desired goals, and outcomes, as well as any other pertinent qualities and characteristics.

Step 2: Create the Application Process

Next, you'll want to create the application and application process. Your certification is not for just anyone who will take it! Have a comprehensive application and review process to ensure that only the best and most qualified applicants are accepted into your certification program. You'll want to identify those who would benefit from sharing your expertise with their clients. Be sure the person you work with is in alignment with your brand and has the same values you do (such as integrity, honesty, and being a servant to others).

Step 3: Get 'em Certified

Now, it's time to host your certification. This will include some type of training—virtual or in-person, one session or day, or multi-session or multi-day? Your process might involve a quiz, demonstration of abilities, or even doing some co-work so they can demonstrate they understand your process.

I hosted my trainings in different ways. I like my certified facilitators and coaches to experience what I'm teaching them. Therefore, I generally provide a two-track certification process. They take the program they are getting certified in, while concurrently learning my thought and execution processes and procedures.

You'll want to design your certification program to fit your particular area of expertise so the recipients can deliver your material with complete confidence.

Make it fun! Under promise and overdeliver. Make that impact!

Step 4: Maintain the Certification (Optional)

If your certification's content is evergreen (meaning it won't change over time or require updated information), you may want to do a one-and-done certification. If you're subject to laws and regulations, you'll want to have a periodic re-certification or at least a review.

You'll also want to ensure that certified individuals remain current in their knowledge and skills by requiring them to complete a reasonable re-certification. This is for their benefit and yours (and your brand's).

Follow these steps to create a certification program that will benefit both your business, the business of those you certify, and those who receive the benefits of everyone's hard work.

In addition, here are some tips to help you commence your certification.

CERTIFICATION PROGRAM – PRACTICAL PRACTICES

Make it Easy to Start

Taking the first step can be the hardest. It's a great idea to make it as easy as possible to take your certification program. Have a clear and concise process for getting started: *What steps do they need to take* (fill out the application, schedule their certification or sign-up dates for your scheduled certifications). Be sure to include what they need to know and what resources are available to help them.

Make the ROI Clear

Your certification program should be valuable to you, your business, and those who get their certification. Carefully consider what skills and knowledge are needed for someone to use your process successfully. In addition, be sure to make the ROI as attractive as possible.

It is absolutely reasonable to charge a fair amount for your certification if using your knowledge and expertise will allow those you certify to experience a measurable increase in their income.

Price it Effectively

Again, your program isn't for everyone. The person who will benefit from using your process should also be able to easily afford to get certified!

Be Flexible and Efficient

The busy professionals you want to certify will have to find time to get certified. Offer a variety of ways to get certified, or at least a variety of times. I certified attorneys on Saturdays and therapists during the workday, usually in the morning.

Have a Great Time!

Did I mention to make it fun? (Yes, I did!) Make sure that your certification program is informational *and* enjoyable. Who wants to sit through a boring class, no matter how much it's going to boost their business? Me, neither. Ensure your program is engaging and interactive, and provides a comprehensive education.

Be Available.

Outside of the formal certification process, I find that being hands-on and available to answer questions and strategize ways to implement the process into my coaches and facilitators' businesses has made a huge difference.

Make it Official.

Once someone has completed their certification, be sure they get a framed certificate (or a certificate they can frame) as proof. Your folks will appreciate it and will proudly display it. It's a fun way to make it official and provide social proof.

HOW TO CHARGE FOR YOUR CERTIFICATION

There are three ways you can charge for and be compensated for certifications:

One-time payment. You can charge for the certification and be done. You can also plan to have a re-certification at the same or a lower fee annually or at the cadence that makes sense.

Payment plus percentage. If your knowledge and expertise are extra valuable, and perhaps if you are providing ongoing support, you may want to charge for the certification plus receive a percentage based on income.

Percentage only. You can also just charge a percentage of income received (I recommend *gross* for obvious reasons, including but certainly not limited to the fact that *net* profits can be manipulated in many ways, but gross revenue is gross revenue).

There are, of course, endless ways to create certifications, provide certification training, and receive compensation. You're limited only to your imagination! Have the best time with this one!

CHAPTER EIGHT

CONSULTING

Consulting is not only in high demand, but it can also be a high-paying income stream.

According to the U.S. Bureau of Labor Statistics, the market is estimated at $250 billion (yes, with a *b*) and is expected to continue its rapid growth.

All of that to say, if you have an area of expertise, chances are there are a *lot* of people who would pay for the fastest path to success in it!

Consulting can be as short as a one-hour, or a multi-hour session, or as long as several years. The best part of consulting (similar to coaching) is you provide your process, and the client does the work.

I've provided consulting around books, specifically how one can publish and position their books for the highest return on the author's time and ROI. If someone wants the road map, I can provide it. That's consulting. I also provide a done-for-you bespoke service where I handle all of the details. Within that service, I provide consulting and strategy so the author assuredly gets the best ROI possible on their investment.

DETERMINE YOUR NICHE

A specialist always makes more than a generalist, and consultants are no different. If you want to command the highest fees, you must first determine what exactly you will provide consulting about.

In addition, be sure to draw clear lines around your consulting to be clear about what you're *not* consulting about!

For example, my specialty is nonfiction. Even more specifically, transformational or prescriptive nonfiction. That means I stay away from memoirs (nonfiction) and anything related to fiction. Yes, even though the fundamentals of publishing professionally also apply to fiction, I send any inquiries to other consultants who help fiction writers or anyone outside of my area of expertise.

You can't be all things to all people, but you can be all things to someone who needs to recreate something you know all about.

Make sense? Good. Now, let's talk about pricing your services.

PRICING YOUR CONSULTING SERVICES

This can be tough to figure out, and if you ask ten consultants what and how they charge, you'll probably get ten different answers. There are several ways you can charge: hourly, on a retainer, flat fee, or value-based.

Hourly. The easiest way to charge is by the hour because this is how other professionals commonly charge. Your client will understand this model, although there might be some pushback on how much time it really takes you—and you might be tempted to not charge the full amount because you think it could be "too much."

However, as a consultant, you are not charging for your time alone. You are providing access to all of your hours of training, education, experience, knowledge, and even previous situational learning.

Retainer. A retainer allows you to receive monthly income for a set number of hours. The upside is you'll know how much revenue you can expect. The downside is that your clients may demand more hours than they've paid for because of this "all-in" option.

Productized Services. You can create a rate sheet your clients can choose from (such as a half-day for a set price or a finished product for an all-in fee). I charge for VIP days, where I provide overview and strategy with valuable take-away assets. I also offer the Better Business Book product for one all-in fee (including ghostwriter, editorial, graphic design, copywriting, and marketing strategy), done in six months. If you have a product you can wrap your arms around in terms of time, costs, and deliverables, consider offering something similar.

Value-Based Pricing. I'm a huge fan of Alan Weiss' value-based fees, which he popularized in a book of the same name. Using the 10x multiple, you charge a fraction of what your client can expect to receive as a return on their investment with you, regardless of how much (or more to the point, how little) time you take to convey your expertise. You charge based on the value of either removing a client's challenge or helping them gain a clear benefit.

Fee from Results. The riskiest of all the models can also result in the highest fees. You are paid based on your client's results. If you do have a coaching or consulting process that you know works, a way to measure your client's progress, and a willing and able client, your chances of success are high. The consultants that succeed are those whose business lasts long enough to make an impact on their clients' lives. And you can only do that if you get pricing right. By familiarizing yourself with the pricing strategies above, you're giving yourself the tools necessary to build a successful moneymaking practice.

With all of these options, you must have clear boundaries and set expectations up front, in writing (including in your agreement). You'll want to avoid common consultant challenges like scope creep, missing deadlines, or other variables that impact the time and effort you spend on a project.

I suggest you do some math and research and then settle on a fee you are absolutely thrilled about.

TIME TO REVENUE?

Like coaching and courses, you can launch a consulting business and retain clients within days or weeks.

CHAPTER NINE

SPEAKING

Speaking can be a fun way to share the contents of your book while simultaneously increasing your book sales (especially if you're able to sell books post-presentation in the back of the room). Speaking allows for expanded impact live and in-person, so it's a fantastic way to gain fans and an increased platform in a short time.

If you love speaking, you'll want to do more of it, and using your book as a launching pad is one very effective way to do just that.

There are a few types of speakers: keynotes and participating on panels are the two I've done most often in my career.

Keynotes are compressed content delivered in a short amount of time that provides inspiration, information, and even transformation.

You can be the opening or closing keynote speaker, or even one of several keynotes.

DESIGNING YOUR KEYNOTE PRESENTATION

There are dozens, maybe hundreds, of ways to create a keynote presentation, all of which provide a structure you can use. You really just have to identify the one that fits with your personality and speaking style. If you're brand new to speaking, you may want to read several of the go-to books on developing a speaking business and hire a speaking or presentation coach to accelerate your progress.

In the meantime, here's a peak into my process:

Know Your Audience. Even if your presentation is a crowd-pleaser with information everyone can use (like time management or stress reduction ideas), do at least some basic research into demographics, background and goals, and current struggles.

Goals. You'll have a goal for your presentation, as will your event's organizer, and so will the audience! Be clear about your goal(s)—do you want to inspire? Entertain? Would you like to position yourself as the thought-leader around your ideas? Know the event organizer's goals: what's bringing the group together, and what is the event's promise to the attendees?

Crafting the speech. When crafting my presentations, I define one main idea and then tend to stick with the Rule of Three: Most people can only take in and remember three pieces of information at one time. Add additional tips or pieces of information, and they get lost or confused (or both).

Come up with three ideas to support the main idea of the presentation and then stick with one, two, or three tips or sub-ideas. This structure provides insight and wisdom that will make your presentation immensely valuable to the audience, especially when you provide takeaways they can use, well, right away.

Keynotes can be as brief as fifteen minutes or as long as ninety. When booking your presentation, you'll probably be asked how long your speech is or, conversely, be told how long you'll have to deliver it.

I've found that having a standard keynote that is incredibly flexible helps me to stick to the time my hosts designate. (It is stressful for the organizer to watch a speaker exceed the time allotted, which throws the entire schedule off.) I can make a presentation longer by sharing stories, shorter by leaving the stories out, or making longer stories shorter.

There are several ways to structure a presentation:

- **Story.** Sharing is a way to create a new reality through story.
- **Roadmap.** This means teaching a new skill or process.
- **Hero's Journey.** Use your own story to help others succeed by sharing your insights and ideas.

I tend to stick with a combination of Roadmap and Hero's Journey.

I've found audiences enjoy—and are grateful for—something tangible they can use in their own lives or businesses. They are either stuck, struggling, or stressed out, and providing my personal recipe combined with something I've overcome has worked well.

You get to decide not only what you want to share but also how to best deliver your content.

Panels. These bring several experts together, usually with a facilitator who asks questions and encourages the audience to ask questions.

You may be on a panel with others who have similar experience or education, or you might talk about topics that are similar. I'm usually at writer's conferences on a panel about publishing. I'm the lone self-publishing expert, along with a hybrid publisher and perhaps an acquisitions editor at a traditional publisher.

Sometimes I don't agree entirely with the positions or opinions of the other panelists, and you might find yourself in the same position. My best advice is to be kind and respectful while sharing your opinion. I'm heavily biased toward self-publishing, but I do think there's a place for traditional and hybrid publishing. Be diplomatic and focus on creating unity rather than division. (Which is, I think, sound advice for any situation, not just participating on a panel!)

PREPPING FOR YOUR PANEL

As an expert, you can simply show up and answer the questions as they come. Most panelists do just that, and it tends to work just fine. To be a crowd-pleaser and give the most to the audience, I suggest you do just a small amount of prep work to enhance your effectiveness on the panel. Crafting these questions and providing them to your facilitator will make their job easier while simultaneously ensuring you know the questions and the answers ahead of time.

TIPS FOR BEING AN AWESOME SPEAKER

You want to be awesome (and memorable in a good way). Said another way, don't be boring! People are trapped, and you don't want the speech you're giving to be the one they can't wait to end!

- **Be engaging.** Ask questions of the audience ("Let me see a show of hands . . ." or "How many of you find . . .") to create interaction and great engagement.
- **Give solid information.** This will solve their problem or give them a way to capitalize on a new opportunity. They want to learn from you, to know what you do and how they can do it, too—just like in your book! Tell them what to do, when, and how, and don't be afraid to be granular in

your advice (I do two Pomodoros every morning to write my book, and I drink black coffee with a lit vanilla-scented candle—something like that.)

- **Share your secret sauce.** Isn't it fantastic when someone opens their kimono and tells you the inside baseball stuff? (I know, right?) I love it when a speaker says, "And here's exactly what I say/do . . ." You'll only endear yourself to your audience, creating raving fans and maybe even future friends in the process.

- **Have a great time, and so will your audience.** Remember, every audience wants every speaker to be magnificent! They want you to be energetic, thought-provoking, and insightful. It may take time to get to the point where you feel as comfortable on stage as you do on your couch, but it's worth the effort. When you're having a ball, your audience will have one as well.

YOUR SPEAKING BUSINESS

Like every other income stream, you need an ideal client, an Agreement, and a way to get paid. Special to speakers is having:

- A One-Sheet. Your one-sheet includes your photo, bio, credentials (hello, authors!), and perhaps awards or a list of previous speaking engagements.

- A Speaker's Reel (or a TED/TEDx talk). I don't have a speaker's reel, but I do have a TEDx talk, *Authenticity is the New Black*, which has served me well for a decade. Event organizers need to see you in action, so put together a short video of you speaking in different situations.

MARKET YOUR SPEAKING BUSINESS WITH YOUR BOOK (AND VICE VERSA)

You can jump-start your speaking business or quickly grow the speaking business you already have with your book. Conversely, you can maximize your book sales by speaking on stages because there's a halo effect on book sales after you complete every presentation.

For New Speakers. If you're a new speaker, start by delivering a couple of dozen free presentations to Rotary or Lions Clubs (and you'll probably sell books as a by-product, but I wouldn't count on making a huge number of sales). While you won't get paid, you'll learn a lot about speaking to different-sized audiences at different times of the day. You'll get a feel for what questions you can answer in the content of your speech over time, while getting comfortable speaking in general and in any situation.

In addition, having "author" on your one-sheet is awesome. It will allow you to command more for your speeches, book more speeches, and (this is the best part) sign and autograph books after you speak.

For Seasoned Speakers. Having a book is a new or another reason to circle back with previous event organizers to see if you can come back. You might be able to make the same presentation or a new one based on the contents of your book. While most organizations won't use the same speaker again for several years, staying in touch never hurts. More times than I can count, relationships like these have resulted in repeat bookings and referrals to other speaking events.

For everyone. When sending your materials to event organizers, either include a physical copy of your book or a link for them to download it (I use BookFunnel to provide digital copies of my book).

In addition, you can offer the option (or make the ask) to sell books in the back of the room after you speak or let them know they can buy multiple copies of the book at a discount (so each attendee gets a copy).

Conferences, summits, and retreats are always looking for great speakers, and being an author and, therefore, an expert on a topic can help you book those speaking engagements more easily than you might think.

Finally, include a full page in the back matter of your book about your speaking. You can title that page: "Book [Insert Your Name] to Speak" with a photo of you on stage and the title of your most popular keynote(s) and direct contact information to your booking agent or assistant.

I've been speaking for more than twenty years, and it is one thing I love to do. You can build a speaking business as big as you want or keep your speaking to a minimum (which is my preference, as I don't love "being on the road."). You get to design your business, this income stream, so you love it—and I hope you do!

TIME TO REVENUE?

Keep in mind that building a professional speaking business and becoming a sought-after speaker, giving dozens of highly paid keynote presentations per year, can take *years* to mature.

However, if keynoting or being on panels doesn't feel like the right fit, I've got another option: training. Come with me to the next chapter, and I'll tell you all about it.

CHAPTER TEN

TRAINING

Training is another great stream of income to add to your empire. If you have content others will benefit from learning, you can build a training business, and customize it to fit your lifestyle.

As a single mom, I truly enjoyed doing keynote speaking but soon realized successful speakers are on the road much of the time. Training allowed me to continue speaking and making an impact, while staying close to home and my daughter. Yet, I was still earning a significant income.

For several years, I provided high-content training for dozens of service firms (law firms, CPA firms, and investment banks, to name a few) on sales and business development.

Eventually, I created a package that combined a day (or two) of training with coaching. I worked with a small group of eight to fifteen within a firm that included at least one full day of training every six months with individual coaching. This provided me with a multi-six-figure income stream that allowed me to earn a great living while still making breakfast and dinner for my daughter and only being away from home a dozen nights per year.

You can design and deliver training based on your book's content combined with other aspects of your knowledge and expertise that are not necessarily included in your book but align with your vision for your life, business, and empire.

The more specialized your training, combined with how much of a problem it solves for your clients, will make you a very much in-demand trainer.

BONUS POINTS FOR BEING AN AUTHOR

Companies love to hire authors who are trainers! It is a true "get" for them—because, as the subject matter expert (SME), you are regarded as someone who can really make a difference.

You'll get extra bonus points for being the author of more than three books in your area of expertise. Additionally, you can charge more for the exact same training someone else who is not an author might deliver.

WHO IS YOUR LEARNER, AND WHAT ARE YOU TEACHING THEM?

First things first, you must define what you're teaching and who exactly your ideal learner would be.

Who is your student? The first step is to define who you are training. As with most income streams, being a specialist (providing training in one specific area of expertise) will allow you to find clients more easily, so be very specific in your ideal client profile.

In the case of training, you have two clients: the managing partner or chief training officer at a firm who will give the green light to hire you, and the actual student who takes your training. I suggest you create a profile for each one.

What do they need to learn? Define *what* they need you to provide in your training.

When I was training service professionals, I knew they came with the base knowledge in their area of expertise. What they needed to learn in order to build a flourishing practice, was how to become rainmakers!

You need to identify their pain points. In my clients' cases—how to develop business consistently—how to manage and even balance their time between developing the business and providing work product. On occasion, they needed to learn how to achieve work-life balance.

Develop an outline for your training and how much time you'll need per module. I developed a seven-hour training called the Rainmaker Bootcamp. I conducted the training in one day, including a working lunch. We started at 9 a.m. and ended promptly at 5 p.m.

I didn't develop it perfectly the first time. In fact, because mine was by request, I interviewed my friend and asked her what the goals of the training would be, then customized the training for her firm. It turned out my subject matter provided pain relief at other firms and other kinds of firms. The initial training I developed was modified, expanded, and changed over the years to adapt to my learners and their needs.

As long as you provide value, your clients will be happy, so feel free to use each training session as a development lab. The more you deliver the content, the more refined and better it will become.

Identify skills and performance gaps. As I mentioned, I interviewed the person who hired me. During each sales conversation with a prospective client, I asked if their firm had the same issues and what other challenges they were having. If it was in my wheelhouse, I added content to support it to my training.

What my students didn't know was how to develop more business in a relationship-based way (my specialty), including where to go to find prospective clients and strategic partners, what language to use to open and close conversations, and how to follow-up. Most of them got their advanced degrees specifically so they wouldn't ever have to sell anything! Surprise, surprise! When they learned that their firms not only wanted them to be competent service providers but also consistent revenue generators (hello, sales!), the stress they felt was palpable.

To solve these problems, I developed a curriculum to help my students understand how to engage new business effectively and efficiently while still having time to execute their work product. All of *this* was so they could enjoy their success (read: not work *all* the time). My training helped them close their knowledge gaps and gave them the confidence to leave my training and immediately put what I taught them into practice.

Once you are clear on your who and what, you'll design your curriculum:

- **Develop a clear goal for your training.** What will your students learn exactly? How long will it take to conduct your training (over how many hours or days)?
- **Clarify success metrics.** How will your students know they can put your training into practice, and how will they know when they've done it correctly?
- **Define the delivery of your training.** In-person? Online? A combination?
- **Craft materials to support your training.** I had a Rainmaker Bootcamp Student Manual I delivered at the beginning of the training. My students could reference it as long as they needed it.

There are resources you can use to guide you through every step of this process, including how to effectively develop a curriculum.

NOW, MARKET YOUR TRAINING

Once you've got a handle on the training you'd like to deliver and who would benefit from it, you get to find clients. This is the fun part—engaging clients and getting signed contracts!

DESIGN YOUR MARKETING STATEMENT.

You'll need to be able to clearly communicate who you train and about what. You'll want to develop a Marketing Statement you can use when someone asks, "What type of training do you deliver?"

My Marketing Statement as a trainer went like this:

I work with service professionals (attorneys, CPAs, bankers, and investment bankers) to help them in their business development efforts. I provide tips, tools, strategies, and ideas so that they can develop more business and become rainmakers.

If I were training authors today, I would say:

I help authors write, publish, and monetize their books by helping them to effectively craft, professionally publish, and turn their books into multiple income streams.

Commit your Marketing Statement to memory and say it over and over until it rolls off your tongue. Remember: confidence conveys, and clarity creates understanding.

TIPS FOR BECOMING AN IN-DEMAND TRAINER

- **Be *the* subject matter expert.** Know every single aspect of your topic *and* be able to communicate about it in a way anyone can understand. Read every article, book, and manual on your area of expertise. Your knowledge will be apparent.

- **Make it easy to hire you.** Have a proposal template ready to send, and when asked, send it within hours.
- **Make it easy to pay you.** Take every type of payment imaginable: checks, wire transfers, credit cards. Be sure to have clear payment parameters.
- **Have a solid sales process.** Identify ideal clients and develop relationships with them over time. Some will be ready today, others not for years. Consistent, persistent, and friendly follow-up is key. While sharpening the skills in your area of expertise, be sure to sharpen your sales skills.
- **Be ready in every way on training day.** Put yourself in a peak state. Said another way, be in a good mood. Avoid being the trainer people are happier to see leave than arrive by being high energy and enthusiastic. Your excitement about your topic will be conveyed to your students, and they will relax and enjoy their time with you because how you're *being* and what they are *learning* will give them the confidence you and your material are really going to help them.

THE BUSINESS OF PROFESSIONAL TRAINING

There are specific materials you'll need to develop a successful training business:

Your master training manual. This is your personal reference, the trainer's manual you'll need to provide your training. You'll create it first (before your student's manual) and then consistently update it with notes, new ideas, and the distinctions you make during and after each delivery or your training. It will prove to be invaluable to you in your business.

Your student's training manual. Your learners will love having something tangible to accompany your training. After you've created your instructor manual, you can use it to develop your students' manual to hand out in conjunction with your training.

You have three options to provide copies to your students, depending upon your clients' wishes and your method of delivery:

- Digital delivery. If you're providing virtual training, you can give the PDF version to your students prior to the training.
- Digital delivery for client printing. On occasion, your client will want to print the files themselves. Again, provide a PDF (and I suggest with password protection) to your client by email or via a file transfer system that they can print.
- Digital delivery for printing. You can send your files to the UPS store closest to the office where you'll be training. You can pick them up prior to the training or arrange for them to be delivered.

YOUR PROPOSAL

For training specifically, you'll want to be clear about certain aspects of your training services. Be sure to include:

- Who do you train, specifically? Is your training for senior-level professionals or brand new hires?
- How many people can attend your training (including minimum and maximum number of participants)?
- How much do you charge (for a training half-day, full day, with or without coaching or consulting)?

SELLING YOUR TRAINING SERVICES

Identify companies and organizations that use trainers in your area of expertise.

Build a bench of other experts who are providing training (in your area of expertise and in others). Referral business can (and should) at some point provide more than eighty percent of your total business.

Use your book to speak to organizations that put you in front of your ideal clients. Chambers of Commerce and Rotary Clubs are always looking for high-content speakers who provide value to their audiences, and you can mention in your presentation (as well as having a note in your bio introduction) that you are a trainer (and what type of training you do). It won't come as a surprise when a member of the audience (or several) approaches you at the end of the meeting (or even emails you shortly thereafter) to find out more about what you offer.

TIME TO REVENUE?

Companies need training—and some training is required! If you specialize in something that requires annual training, even better! Regardless, once you've created your training, you can engage a client relatively quickly, depending upon your marketing initiatives.

CHAPTER ELEVEN

TURN YOUR BOOK INTO A BOOK SERIES

You've written your book and might think that's the end. In fact, you might not have yet considered your option to craft a series of books around your expertise.

Or, maybe you have but don't know how or where to start.

I've written several series and have found that not only does it make me happy to do them, but readers love 'em, too!

SERIES OPTIONS

Let's dive into the different options, and along the way, I'll share some key distinctions for each type of series:

LINEAR

A book series that is linear takes the reader on a journey by approaching each aspect of a topic one phase at a time. Each book has a specific purpose and addresses one aspect of the reader's journey on a topic.

First example: I wrote the *Like a Boss* series with Ben Hale. Ben is a successful middle-grade fantasy author. We wrote three books in the series, *Write Like a Boss, Publish Like a Boss,* and *Market Like a Boss,* and then published one big book, an omnibus, with all three books included. Each of us wrote in our areas of expertise (fiction or nonfiction) and noted the logical crossover points. We even used different fonts so readers would be sure to know who was writing which section.

We employed a fairly rapid release strategy, publishing the books two months apart and then the omnibus about a year after the third individual book was published.

I've employed the same strategy with the first book in this book's series, *You Must Write a Book,* followed by *You Must Market Your Book.* With each book, I also published a companion workbook.

ONE SUBJECT BY TOPIC

Perhaps your book's topic would benefit those in a group, one particular area of discipline, or profession. *The Miracle Morning* book series started with one book and was expanded over a half-dozen years to include titles for professionals (entrepreneurs, salespeople, network marketers, teachers, writers) and groups (parents and college students). We even published a coloring book for adults and kids!

If you have a general topic that would help those in a niche, consider curating your content with a book specific to them.

The model of *The Miracle Morning* books was to take the foundational information, (the Life SAVERS, which are: *silence, affirmations, visualization, exercise, reading,* and *scribing*), customized for each topic. In addition, we included detailed information to help the individual reader be the best they could be. We partnered with SMEs who customized the consistent content and then provided insight into their particular area of expertise.

MULTIPLE ASPECTS

Another option is to create a series that explores each aspect or angle of a topic, one book at a time.

I've done this twice myself:

The Prosperous Writer book series started with *Prosperity for Writers*. By request, I created *The Prosperous Writer's Productivity Journal*, then partnered with my author buddy, Brian Meeks, to write *The Prosperous Writer's Guides to Making More Money, Finding Readers*, and *The Nifty 15: Write Your Book in Just 15 Minutes a Day*.

The Successful Single Mom series started with the original book, and then I realized there were other challenges single moms faced (finding love again, staying fit, feeding their kids healthy, nutritional meals because they are stretched thin, going back to school, and making enough money to pay for everything), so I made a list and wrote a book to help them solve each of those problems:

- *The Successful Single Mom Cook! Cookbook*
- *The Successful Single Mom Gets Rich!*
- *The Successful Single Mom Gets Fit!*
- *The Successful Single Mom Finds Love!*
- *The Successful Single Mom Gets an Education*

And I had a blast writing each of them. Having a series allowed my busy, single mom readers (whom I understood very well with six years as a single mom myself) to read the book(s) they needed to read. Yes, there's an omnibus of them as well.

I think I've tackled series in every way I could think of, but I'm sure there are many others that haven't occurred to me. As with every income stream, you're only limited to your imagination.

A FEW WORDS ABOUT COAUTHORING

I've had an absolute blast writing books with coauthors. Writing can be a lonely journey, but having someone to collaborate with, bounce ideas off, and share a giggle or two here and there can be fantastic. Not to mention, it's fun, and you get to know someone well in the process.

Of course, it is not always rainbows and unicorns. Retaining a budding or long-time friendship should be a consideration (it always is for me), so here are a few tips to make sure you're as happy a decade from now as you were when you first hit upon the idea of working with someone:

- **Define your roles and responsibilities.** Who is writing which parts, what are the goals, and how is the book getting published (and if you're self-publishing, who's paying for what), marketed, etc.? Put it in writing and then remember . . .

- **Good fences make good neighbors—and coauthors.** *Before* you write the words, have your attorney draft an agreement with clear expectations based on who is doing—and paying for—what. Very few things sour a relationship faster than miscommunication, or one person feeling like they've done the lion's share of the work. Clarity is power, and talking through the what ifs and who's gonna will keep everything smooth sailing.

- **Have a schedule and stick to it—or be awesome and renegotiate your agreement.** I think this is a fundamental idea for life, and it definitely applies here! I've been working on a coauthor project recently, and much to my chagrin, I've had some personal challenges, and I got sick. Both of them threw me off my schedule, leaving my coauthor waiting for my writing. I called myself out, apologized, and set a new deadline. Fortunately, she's awesome, and we're good. It probably wouldn't be that way if I'd avoided the topic or not owned up to it.

THE BUSINESS OF BOOK SERIES

If you're doing your own series, keep these ideas in mind:

- You'll want your covers to "go" (not match but go together so readers realize there's a series). Have them designed by the same designer; it's even better if you have them done all around the same time.

- Utilize the series options when publishing that are available on retail platforms (another way to establish each book is as part of a series).

If you're working with a coauthor, the above applies, and you'll also want to be sure to:

- Include them in the major decisions. This might not apply if you're going to retain the ownership and they are simply contributing their part.

- However, if you're truly coauthoring, keep in mind you'll be paying royalties forever (until the books stop selling). Someone will have to continue payments until seventy years after the death of the last coauthor.

- Consider paying outright for your coauthor's contribution, or engage an accountant to make those monthly or quarterly payments.

Series are a fantastic way to keep book sales going, as well as build your catalog of books. Now that I truly understand the power of a series, I encourage you to give it a close look if writing books is something you enjoy.

TIME TO REVENUE?

Books, as we know, take time. You can launch the first or next book in your series as quickly as you can produce a quality book—on the fast track, four to six months (if some of the content is re-used), to up to a year on a more reasonable schedule (especially if you're writing completely new content).

CHAPTER TWELVE

SELLING BOOKS IN BULK AND CUSTOM PRINTING

Selling books individually is fantastic—you'll love making the sale and collecting your profit. Even more fun is selling a book and getting the opportunity to sign it to the recipient.

More fun? Bulk sales! Selling a bunch of books all at the same time, exponentially increases your income and your impact in one transaction.

While not part of my original plan, making bulk book sales is (and has always been) one of my surprise favorite income streams in my empire.

SELLING BOOKS IN BULK

If you have a book that's a crowd-pleaser, chances are there are individuals, groups, and companies who will want to buy and give away your books to their networks or employees.

Selling in bulk actually all started back at the beginning of my publishing journey. To gain traction for their first book, Mark Victor Hansen and Jack Canfield focused on doing seven things every day to sell their first *Chicken Soup for the Soul* book. I attended an event Mark hosted in the early 2000s called Mega Book Marketing. I remember vividly when he was on stage talking about their book marketing initiatives. He talked about how they were able to sell so many copies of their first book: They asked every person they met if they wanted to buy between ten and one hundred copies of their book. It worked!

It's been too long, and I don't remember how many copies they initially sold. Suffice it to say that tactic worked wonders, so I figured I might as well use it myself.

Print-on-demand wasn't available then, so I used an independent printer to order my books. The big price break came when I ordered 5,000 books (which, at the time, was right over $4,000). I bit the bullet and ordered my first 5,000 books and then really felt the pressure to sell them!

Using Mark and Jack's questions, I was able to sell 11,000 copies of the original *Tall Order! Organize Your Life and Double Your Success in Half the Time* in just three weeks by calling everyone I knew. Eventually, I raised the stakes and started asking folks to buy between one hundred and one thousand books. Most folks ordered ten books; some ordered twenty-five or fifty. However, several of my coaching clients had companies with thousands of people, and I had several multi-thousand book orders.

It was pretty cool to cross the ten thousand books sold number and place my third order for five thousand books in just a few weeks. Then I had an "oh snap!" moment, realizing I would have to take delivery of those books and then turn around and deliver or send them to the recipients. Suffice it to say I took a break from making sales calls to tally up my profits and start printing labels and buying envelopes and boxes so I could fulfill the orders!

Today, bulk book orders are still a fun and profitable part of my business, and your options for order fulfillment are plentiful and easier.

Present day, there are a few ways bulk books are sold in my business.

One-to-Many

The Successful Single Mom and *If Divorce is a Game* books are popular with divorce attorneys, therapists, and certified divorce financial advisors. *Vision to Reality* and *Business Dating* are used in executive and business coaching practices.

Individuals order the books and share them with their clients and prospective clients.

I give my first price break at twenty-five books, giving a ten to twenty percent discount or more as the orders get bigger.

Some-to-Many

Organizations, including companies and associations, use books to grow or enhance their sphere of influence (sales teams, executive teams, employees, or strategic partners).

Many of them have book clubs and are actively looking for books to purchase and love when the author can show up for a live (or virtual) Q&A.

In 2018, I flew to San Francisco and did a live worldwide event for a Fortune 100 company, talking to people in dozens of countries around the world for over two hours. *That* was fun! The company paid for my time and travel and bought twenty-five hundred books months in advance so they could be shipped around the world before the event.

The Miracle Morning for Teachers and *The Miracle Morning Art of Affirmations Coloring Book* have been ordered in bulk since shortly after the COVID pandemic graced us with its presence in 2020. Schools, and eventually school systems, recognized the mental health issues brought on by increased stress and isolation and have been actively seeking social-emotional learning and support tools. Enter *The Miracle Morning* Life SAVERS practice. Teachers used it in classrooms with their students. Then, the school principals started using a six-minute school-wide practice every morning. These books, along with several others in the series, help provide a structure that alleviates stress and produces feelings of well-being and happiness. Attendance (students, teachers, and faculty) increased, and bullying, fighting, detentions, and expulsions decreased. When writing and publishing those books, the intended outcome was impact, but none of the coauthors could foresee *how* the impact would take place. We've followed the breadcrumbs, and it's a great idea for you to do that as well.

You'll want to identify who could use your book to make progress on their goals, help them look better, feel better, get more business, or handle difficult or stressful situations. Then, identify where you can connect with them. Since I obviously don't know what kind of book you have, here are some ideas:

- If your book has inspirational stories of people who have made it through tough times, you could sell your books to hospitals so they can give them to their patients.
- If your book is about time management, speak to organizations that have busy, stressed executives. In addition to or in lieu of a speaking fee, they will want to buy books for the attendees.
- If your book provides a path to building financial freedom through entrepreneurship, focus on organizations that serve professionals who have those golden handcuffs (big salaries and the expensive lifestyle to go with them).

I suggest using a whiteboard or an extra-large Post-it note (think about the ones the size of a standing whiteboard you can put on the wall) and brainstorm at least ten ideas for how to sell your books in bulk. Here are some questions that can help:

- What is the profile of some of your book's readers (age, occupation, pain points, etc.), and what positive feedback have they given you? *This will allow you to succinctly share how your book helps.*
- What was your book's original avatar, and who serves them? *Is there a governing body that would buy and distribute books (maybe they would even be required reading)?*
- Where does your avatar hang out? *Associations, conferences, organizations, clubs, and groups all provide the opportunity to sell books.*

CUSTOM PRINTING

There's another option for selling books in bulk that is absolutely next-level and can boost your empire by yet one more income stream: custom printing (also known as white-labeling.) Here you allow your client to change one or several aspects of your book to suit their needs.

Custom Printing Options

Front cover. They can add a graphic seal (think sunburst) to the front of the book that says, *A Gift from Turner & Smith, LLP.* This can be added by your graphic designer, or gold seals can be printed and added separately.

One company bought three thousand copies of one of my books, had their admin team add the seals, and put them in their annual conference gift bags.

Another firm wanted a custom cover, and we printed ten thousand copies with their logo inside a gold seal on the front.

Back cover. The easiest customization is when you limit it to the back cover. Typically, you'll have your sales copy on the back of the book—why someone should *buy* it. Since it is now a gift, the back cover is now available real estate your client can use to sell their business instead.

They can add their logo, a photo of the principles in the business, a description of their company, and even a testimonial or two. Included in the set-up fee is the design of their choosing.

Inside content. While most of my custom printed books have been with back cover customization, a client will occasionally request changing something about the inside of the book. You can decide if you want to make that an option, and you'll charge accordingly.

For example, in one version of the original *Tall Order!*, my client requested we include a note from the Chairman of the Board about why he loved the book, wanted everyone to read it, and how they were implementing some of the ideas.

CHARGING FOR CUSTOM PRINTED BOOKS

Bulk sales allow large quantities of books to be ordered at a lower price per book than retail.

The same applies to custom books. However, you'll want to charge a set-up fee (I started at $1,000, but now it is much higher) and a separate fee for each change.

You can charge a set-up and design fee, and a separate charge if they want to change *anything* on the inside of the book (keep in mind you'll have to have the writing edited and proofed and the new version of those book files (cover and interior) designed as if from scratch), on the front cover or the back cover. Make those charges à la carte—they can choose one or all of them.

CONTRACTS AND ORDER FORMS, INVOICES AND RECEIPTS, PRINTING AND FULFILLMENT

Bulk orders and custom printing require some preparation and planning, as well as an understanding of the process from both the salesperson's side (that's you) and the buyer.

- **Contracts and Order Forms:** You don't necessarily need a contract for bulk book sales, but you most certainly do for custom printing, and you need an order form for both. On your form, include price breaks (i.e., order two hundred and fifty books, receive a five percent discount off the retail price, five hundred books, ten percent, etc.). Having a lower price for larger quantities encourages larger orders.

- **Invoices and Receipts:** When an order is placed, you'll want to send an invoice (or have your accountant or bookkeeper do that for you), as well as a receipt that the order has been paid for. In some instances, books must be received for payment to be issued. You'll have to decide whether you can handle these types of orders—in some instances, bulk orders have six-figure pricing. Order fifty thousand or one hundred thousand books, and your printer will want payment prior to printing. You'll have to have a way to pay for it and then wait thirty, sixty, or sometimes even ninety days for your money; however, when you pay $3 to $5 per book, including tax and shipping, and your customer pays $10 and up for the books, that's a wonderful return on that short-term wait. (If you don't have a few hundred thousand dollars lying around, you can look for short-term financing through companies that provide factoring. Invoice factoring companies connect businesses with the cash they need by purchasing their outstanding invoices and assuming responsibility for collections. Factoring companies are often more concerned with the creditworthiness of a business's customers, so this source of financing is ideal for businesses with less established credit). Finally, once the order has been paid in full, be sure to provide a receipt (and keep a digital and physical copy for your files, just in case).

- **Printing and Fulfillment:** You have some choices when it comes to fulfillment. For bulk orders of 999 and under, you can use Amazon or Ingram Spark with Draft2Digital and Barnes & Noble also provides print-on-demand (POD) options. You'll pay the same amount per book for one book or 999 books. There are also independent printers who produce books and are less expensive once you get to a certain order count (usually 200 to 300 books). Independent printers become the better option for the more books you're ordering. You might recall I paid $4000 for five thousand books "back in the day," and that's because four thousand books were $1.10 each ($4,400). I got an additional thousand books for $400 less. While you don't want to warehouse books, sometimes ordering a large quantity and sending them yourself could make sense; however, both POD and independent printers will ship directly to your customer. You provide and receive payment; they do the heavy lifting. (Which, in my opinion, is magical and makes this a great income stream to focus your energies on!) One last thought on printing and fulfillment: You'll want to stay on top of your customer's shipments and ensure all books are received. Sometimes, the number of books shipped isn't the number received, and your customer will want all the books they paid for (and they will count them!). A few thousand books (out of hundreds of thousands) have been ordered twice. Where the missing books ended up is a mystery. Make your customers happy, and someday, they will probably order more books.

MORE IMPORTANT DETAILS

Design and Customization Options: Cover and Interior

Your clients won't know what they don't know, so be clear before commencing your marketing on this topic what you will—and won't—allow in terms of your book's customization.

- Can they change individual chapters around? Add a Foreword or a call to action in the back?

- Just be cognizant of the fact that when you do books in this way, your brand is inextricably linked to their brand—do they go together?

- Do you want to offer the "anything you want" option or limit them to a front cover seal or back cover design?

Marketing

Books at rest are money at rest, and the last thing you and your clients want is a stack of boxes with books in them collecting dust. I created a marketing plan to help my clients get their books—and, therefore money—in motion. Once they've bought the books, the best thing for them is to get them into the hands of their employees, prospective clients, or strategic partners.

You'll want to help them circulate the books in whatever way makes sense, depending on the reason they've purchased the books. Brainstorm some ideas and help them make good use of the books, not simply buy them.

Your clients may want to use front cover graphics in their emails and websites, especially if they are using the books to market their businesses, so be sure to get front cover and square jpegs for them.

One last suggestion: Recommend or even buy BookFunnel and provide a digital copy of their book (yes, you can charge more for this, but you might not want to—goodwill and great karma and all that). They can share digital copies with whomever they like, which will help them get a great return on their investment with you.

Customer Service

In addition to ensuring receipt of their entire order and helping them to make the most of their purchase, you'll want to develop a relationship with your clients. Check in with them from time to time to see how things are going and what feedback they are getting about the books.

When you receive custom and bulk orders, it might be months or even years in between orders. Be sure to stay in touch over time with your clients; you never know when they'll make another order, and you want to be top of mind when they're ready (i.e., you wouldn't want them not to be able to reach you because they couldn't remember your name or didn't have your email address handy).

As is the case of several income streams in this book, the sky is the limit with ways to sell custom and bulk books.

TIME TO REVENUE?

There's no short answer here—it took me just a few weeks to sell bulk copies of my first book, and a few years to develop relationships (plus marketing processes for myself and my clients) with the right organizations to make recurring bulk sales. If this is an area of interest, though, it can be lucrative if you stick with it.

CHAPTER THIRTEEN

VIRTUAL SUMMITS

Virtual summits are an interesting and, in many cases, extremely profitable way to monetize your book.

While I don't consider myself an expert on summits, I have a unique perspective on them because I've been a guest on many (many!) of them, and I've hosted my own (twice): the Empire Builders Summit. Full disclosure: the total *direct* income in the form of premium pass sales has not generated six-figures for my empire; the *indirect* income has been substantial, which is why I think they are worthy of a mention in this book.

Please note since I am *not* a virtual summit expert, you'll want to connect with someone who specializes in summits if you want help or even a done-for-you service. In this chapter, I'm sharing an overview plus my perspective and experience. You'll definitely want to do your research and dig deeper into how effective and profitable summits take place.

WHAT IS A VIRTUAL SUMMIT?

Virtual summits are gatherings of industry experts and thought leaders who share their knowledge, expertise, and insights over one or more days.

People love watching summits to get a great education on a topic in a short period of time, while discovering new experts they didn't know before.

You can center your virtual summit around your book's content, or you can do what I did and pull the lens back and focus on a broader topic.

They consist of live or recorded interviews between the host and expert guests. On your landing page, you'll give access for the best price for your Premium Passes (usually $59 or $69) with lifetime access to all of the interviews.

My Summits

I pre-recorded the interviews with about twenty guests for my first summit, then recorded a dozen new interviews the second time around.

My summits lasted five days (Monday through Friday), with a live kick-off on Monday and a bonus live Q&A on Saturday. I divided the number of interviews by five. I gave access on Monday to Monday's interviews. On Tuesday, I gave access to Monday and Tuesday's interviews. Then, on Wednesday, to Tuesday and Wednesday's interviews, and so on. Over the weekend, there was full access to all of the interviews.

WHY HOST A VIRTUAL SUMMIT?

Virtual summits are a fantastic way to:

- **Build your expert standing.** You get to interview the other experts in your area of expertise *and* invite the ones you don't know (who will probably say yes). Being seen as the leader of a group of experts is a solid way to build name, face, and brand recognition.
- **Build your email list.** Email is still the best way to communicate with your audience and prospective clients.

Virtual summits are a great way to grow your list.
- **Build a new income stream (or two).** Tickets to your virtual summit will most likely be free, but access is limited. Some participants will want unlimited, forever access to your summit and will be willing to pay for a premium pass, and others will want your "big ticket offer."
- **Boost your other income streams.** Chances are you have developed or are developing the other income streams in this book, and your summit can expose your offerings to your participants, increasing their profitability as well.

These are just a few reasons why hosting a virtual summit is worth considering.

MY SUMMITS

I interviewed only people I knew well for my summits, including colleagues who have empires with multiple income streams, and participants in the Empire Builders Mastermind. You can invite people you know and people you don't. Just make sure they'll add value to your attendees, and you add value to them with your conversation!

The direct income from both of my summits (individually) was around $15,000, but the exposure to my courses and the Empire Builders Mastermind was over six-figures in my first two years.

HOW TO HOST A VIRTUAL SUMMIT

There are a lot of moving parts to hosting a summit. Here's a list of what you'll need to effectively host yours:
- **A landing page.** You'll want one specific page for your summit on your website or learning management service (LMS) with fantastic sales copy, of course. You'll also create individual day landing pages.

- **A hosting platform.** Choose how you'll deliver your summit. I originally used Kartra but moved everything over to Thinkific (as that's where my courses "live"). Having one fully functional platform is helpful and cost-effective.
- **Video recording equipment and an application.** I use a Lavalier mike, a 4K camera, and Zoom to record my live videos and QuickTime Player to record my solo videos.
- **Guest information and spreadsheet.** You'll need each guest's photo, bio, and a few sentences about their session and why participants won't want to miss it. Keep a spreadsheet with everything in it, and use that information to build your daily landing pages.
- **An email service.** You can use one like ConvertKit, Aweber, or MailChimp, plus an email sequence to build interest in your summit.
- **Social media assets (graphics and copy).** Use these to drive sign-ups.

My Summits

I worked with Ray Brehm for my summit, and he made the delivery of each day's content to my participants a breeze. It is a lot of admin work to put the summit together, but once it's done, you can run your summit on repeat once, twice, or even a few times a year (or make it an evergreen option).

CREATING YOUR SUMMIT CONTENT

The interviews. The content of your summit, provided by your experts, is a critical part of making your summit a must-watch.

- Determine how long your interviews will be. *I kept mine to 20-30 minutes and asked just a half-dozen questions (which I provided prior to the interview).*

- Make a list of experts you want to interview for your summit. Invite them via email with insight into how long they need to be available and provide them with your questions. *A simple call, text, or email is effective for invitations.*
- Schedule a few days to record interviews and provide a link to your calendar so your experts can easily schedule themselves. *I scheduled back-to-back thirty-minute interviews with a buffer in between, which enabled me to finish all of my interviews in just a few days.*

My Summit

Some summit hosts require their guests to email *their* lists about the summit. I didn't do that because I felt like if they wanted to email their list, they would—but their presence was their present to me and my participants. I don't like the "you must email your list every day" requirements some hosts have. But I'll mention it in one or two of my daily emails.

You get to decide what rules you want to have around your summit and guest experts. My suggestion is that you make it easy to say yes to you and hard to say no.

NEXT: YOUR SUMMIT

I loved the experience of having my own summits (and will continue to have them) and being a guest on other experts' summits, and I think you will, too. Do your research, plan it out, and go for it! You never know where those magical conversations or connections with other experts or participants will take you!

TIME TO REVENUE?

Putting together a summit can take a few months, but you can start realizing revenue the minute you put your landing page up with a link to upgrade to the paid ticket.

CHAPTER FOURTEEN

MASTERING YOUR MASTERMIND

This might be my favorite chapter and income stream of all. Hosting my mastermind, the Empire Builders Mastermind (EBM), for the past five years has been, in a word, the *best*.

If you're reading this chapter, chances are you've at least contemplated the idea (or you saw this chapter and wanted to get the scoop).

WHAT IS A MASTERMIND?

A mastermind is a peer-to-peer group designed to help members capitalize on opportunities and solve problems with input and advice from the other group members, led by someone with knowledge and expertise.

Masterminds come in all shapes, sizes, make-ups, and price points. There are small two and three-person masterminds, and there are some with hundreds of people. The focus of a mastermind can be narrow or broad. The investment for participants can be negligible or considerable.

As the host, you get to decide all of it!

WHO SHOULD HOST A MASTERMIND?

Once you've published your book, chances are you're fielding inquiries from readers asking you to go deeper, and answer complex questions you couldn't address in your book. Hosting a mastermind can be an incredible way to deepen your impact on others.

If you have extensive knowledge about a topic and the desire to work closely with others who want to benefit from that expertise, a mastermind might be the perfect way to do just that!

WHAT TO CONSIDER WHEN FORMING YOUR MASTERMIND.

The decision to launch a mastermind must be preceded by careful thought and consideration. With forethought, your mastermind can be a win-win for you and your participants. Without forethought, you could have unforeseen challenges. Kindly allow me to help!

Here are a few things to determine *before* you announce your mastermind:

- **What is the main focus of your mastermind, and what is the promise?** You'll want a clear purpose. The purpose of EBM is to help participants build multiple streams of income (one of them is a book). I've built more than a dozen income streams and have extensive experience that can both help EBMers avoid pain (financial, personal, emotional, and in their business) and capitalize on opportunities faster and easier than without my guidance.

- **What will you name it?** Just like titling your book, make it clear what the group is about.

- **How often will you meet (weekly or monthly)? How and where will you meet (virtually or in-person or both)?** EBM kicks off in-person in December, meets eleven months a year, and in-person for the mid-year meeting in June. We are dark in August and have our last virtual meeting in November.

- **How long is your "term" (six months? A year?), and how often is it open for enrollment?** I seat the following year's EBM class all year, with most enrollments taking place between August 1st and October 31st.
- **What type of person is the ideal participant?** Craft an ideal participant profile (and trust me, over time, you'll refine this to narrow it down).
- **How many people do you want in your mastermind?** I keep EBM small—around fifteen people. I started with six and have grown as the years have gone by. Yet I don't foresee ever having more than twenty people in the group.
- **Will they have access to you outside of your regular, structured meetings, and if so, how much? How will they schedule time with you?** I allow almost unlimited access to me by my participants—I provide a scheduling link so they can get on my calendar, or they can just email, call, or text. This is highly unusual (and not necessarily recommended). However, in EBM my participants sometimes need real-time advice, and it can be a challenge to get on my schedule. My promise is that I'll connect with them as soon as I possibly can, and I might be multi-tasking (taking a walk, driving, etc.).
- **How much will you charge each participant?** My advice here is the lawyer's answer: it depends. Based on all of the other answers, you'll want to charge a fee that is enough so they pay attention, and you feel well-compensated for the time, money, and effort you put into the group.

While it is a fantastic way to increase your income, with that increase comes other considerations.

- **The members of your mastermind will look to you for leadership, coaching, and mentorship.** You need to have a reserve of time and energy. The coaching and mentorship that comes with hosting a mastermind takes a lot of both, and you need to have them to give. It is better to under promise and overdeliver than the opposite.

- **Having a mastermind requires more preparation time than you initially (and ever) think.** You need white space to think through and organize gatherings and events, who you want to invite to be in your mastermind, and execute everything as though it were simple and easy. When you do it well, you'll find members stick around for longer than one term.

- **Selection is key.** *Selection* of members is critical—they need to be easy for you to work with and easy for them to gel with each other. *Selection* of a topic for your mastermind allows you to stay focused. *Selection* of the meeting dates, times, locations, and even extras like food that work for everyone will only add exponentially to the quality and the end result.

MOVING FORWARD.

As you can see, there is a lot to think about when it comes to a mastermind, but I can honestly say every single aspect is worth it. The hours spent putting together in-person events, crafting special presentations, having discovery calls with prospective members, scouting locations, and every other little detail is one hundred percent worth it. It took me a few years to get it (mostly) figured out, and I honestly love every minute of it. In case you're wondering why, exactly, it's because I get to closely mentor those who want to create an empire they own (that doesn't own them), and they are open to the coaching and mentoring I can provide. It gives me great pleasure to help those I work with to create what they want with little (or no) pain and suffering, and much faster than I was able to figure it out on my own.

Because this is just one chapter of a book and because I didn't have the mastermind when I created the Building a Million Dollar Business course, I created a separate course you might be interested in, Build a Six-Figure Mastermind. The course is fully comprehensive where this chapter simply cannot be—and if you're seriously considering hosting your own, it would be a wise investment. In the meantime, I hope I've answered a lot of the questions you had, and I also really hope you host a mastermind because you will love it!

TIME TO REVENUE?

There are two answers here: First, you can earn revenue on your first mastermind fairly quickly (within a few weeks or months). Second, you will earn far more revenue over time once you've (a) hosted a popular mastermind people want to join and (b) refined your processes. My mastermind, in 2024, is in its sixth year and is exponentially more profitable for me than it was in years one through four.

SECTION III

MONEY IN MOTION

CHAPTER FIFTEEN

CHOOSING YOUR BEST AND FASTEST PATH TO REVENUE

You've come this far, and chances are you're trying to choose which income stream to do first. I'd lay some money on the fact you have more than one you want to work on, and you're wondering which one to choose first or whether you can work on more than one at a time.

I know, I feel you: *so many ideas, so little time.*

It's okay; take a deep breath. Let's circle back to how to decide which idea to focus on first (as well as how to put them in order and create a future production schedule).

In Chapter Three, I suggested you ask yourself a few questions before choosing a revenue stream to launch. Now that you've read through the choices presented in this book and have insight into how long it could take each income stream to provide cash flow, you can marry your timetable to the best income stream to launch now. Then, you can define your longer-term schedule for building out the others you want to put in place.

TIMELINE: WHAT'S YOUR URGENCY?

Remember how long it took to go from blank page to book launch? Yup, it's not a quick turnaround—probably around a year. As you already know, professionally publishing a quality book isn't the fastest path to revenue.

Different income streams can produce markedly different results, and the timelines can vary just as much. So, back to you—how soon do you need to see the numbers in your bank account increase? If you need money *now*, you will want to choose something that has a faster return on your time investment than if you don't.

There are some points to consider about your timeline, *especially* if you're in a hurry to make money.

More Time, More Money, More Effort

I want to point out (again) that while some income streams can generate income in just a few hours or even days, it will almost always take longer, cost more, and require more effort than you initially thought. Making accurate projections isn't necessarily my strong suit, and it's challenging to do that, even for the best in business.

My very non-scientific approach is this: I take any expectations (about time, money, energy, and effort) I have based on experience and common sense and multiply them by 1.5 (one-point-five). If I think I need to spend $100 on something, I budget $150. I'm thrilled if it costs less, but I'm ready to invest more. With that expanded view, I'm usually thrilled with the results. One of the reasons I wrote this book was to save you time, money, and effort—I want you to get results faster, with less out-of-pocket expense, and easier than I have.

However.

You'll still want to set reasonable yet aggressive expectations and then keep going until you get your intended results.

Keep in mind, some income streams take a significant amount of time before you see a measurable return; however, they will be in place forever. Be sure to understand you are trading time for money, not in the traditional sense of getting paid by the hour, but that you have to put in at least some time to get paid now, later, or both. Books and courses are examples of longer-term payoffs. They take time to create and, done well, can pay you forever (especially if they contain evergreen content).

Choose the income stream(s) that factors into your longer-term success as soon as you can, even if you have to choose a more rapid path today. Then, keep chipping away at all of them until they are in place and making money. Be sure to market them consistently for as long as it makes sense.

EMBRACE THE ELF: EASY, LUCRATIVE, AND FUN

As I mentioned, before you decide which income stream to develop, you'll want to think through the concepts of *easy*, *lucrative*, and *fun*. In addition to how *fast* you need to make money, not all income streams are created equal.

Easy

Some income streams are easier than others—and please let me be the first person to tell you to make *everything* as easy on yourself as possible. While not all aspects of each income stream are easy, err on the side of choosing the stream you find to be easier than others. Writing a book is hard for some people, easy for me. That's why I keep doing it. Just because something is easy, doesn't mean you shouldn't make a lot of money doing it! Isn't that the point anyway? Find what you can do that's easy and monetize the heck out of it!

But to be clear, I wouldn't just focus on the easy money aspect. Some income streams are just easier to deliver, and that will depend on you, your experience, and your desire to execute a particular stream.

Not all aspects of any income stream are rainbows and lollipops. There are many elements of different income streams I don't love, but when I can love eighty percent or more, and not love twenty percent or less, I do it.

Lucrative

Of course, you want to choose income streams that will be lucrative. Lucrative can be closely related or completely unrelated to time—just as it can be unrelated to easy and fun.

Circling back to the time element and staying on the topic of writing a book, let's talk about how lucrative books can be. I laugh now when people tell me their perception is that you can't make money from books. *Of course*, you can, and many do! But no one decides to write, publish, and monetize their book and does it inside of a few months (at the very fastest). Books can be incredibly lucrative, but they take time to do well. And, of course, monetizing them in the most lucrative fashions can be a life-long effort (and one well worth it, I might add).

Courses and coaching, to name two, can be very lucrative, both in the short and long-term. But if you don't want to put in the time to produce a quality course, it doesn't matter how lucrative it could be. You'll fail to get the results you want if you don't do it well, initially and over time. If you don't like people, you won't be a great coach, so it won't matter that you can outline a great coaching program in an afternoon and put up a landing page in a couple of days. You won't like it, and it won't be lucrative.

Fun

The last of these three qualifiers, just like the first two, is subjective. What you consider fun and what I consider fun could be completely different! There are many income streams you won't find in this book because I either haven't done them yet or I've taken a hard look and made a hard pass.

No matter how long you live, life is too short not to enjoy what you're doing—*including building your empire.*

It must be fun, at least most of the time, or your rate of success (if you succeed at all) will be low. Or, you must accept the non-fun parts of the income stream because the payoff is worth it.

If you love to create courses but hate putting in the hours to create a quality product, or you hate marketing and sales, it's probably a colossal waste of time to do courses.

If you love to speak but detest marketing your speaking business, spending a lot of time on airplanes (read: in airports) or strange beds, maybe training is a better option.

I sandwiched lucrative between easy and fun because while it is about the money, it is never *only* about the money. Be sure to focus on income streams that check all of the boxes, not just one. You want your chosen income streams to feel like a dream come true.

It doesn't matter how easy, lucrative, or even fun an income stream could be; if you don't want to do it, do not do it.

> **ONE MAN'S TRASH IS ANOTHER MAN'S TREASURE—
> ONE PERSON'S FAVORITE INCOME STREAM
> COULD BE ANOTHER PERSON'S NIGHTMARE.**

CHOOSING

If you're like me, you want all of the income streams and right now would be great! In my experience, you will have the highest success rate if you choose just one or two to start with. (See my thoughts on long-term income stream strategic planning below).

When I have two streams or projects I want to work on, I analyze them using the same qualifiers I've given you, with some additional forethought:

- How does it fit into my long-term plan? *My goal is one or two new income streams per year, preferably the ones I work on for a period of time, to earn money for at least a decade.*

- How easy will it be to add production time to my schedule? *I can do everything, just not all at once. I calculate the number of hours I think I'll need to get it done and add blocks of time to my calendar.*

- How long will it take me to recoup my investment, and what are the one, five, and ten-year potential returns on my investment? *I want to get in the black as soon as possible and continue to reap the rewards over the long-term.*

- How much time, money, and energy do I need to devote to it, once it's in place, for marketing, business development, content, etc.? *Even books—especially books—require long-term love (marketing) if the goal is for them to provide a high return. Choose a stream you have a passion for that can stand the tests of time, and lack of profitability (at least at first), that you enjoy.*

- Once the hard part is done, can the income streams be as ELF as possible for the foreseeable future? *It's easier to swallow how hard something can be to put in place if the long-term return is rosy.*

LONG-TERM STRATEGIC PLANNING AND EXECUTION

I keep a running list of income streams I want to develop (I have yet to host in-person writing retreats or monetize my podcast), books I want to write, and other goals related to expanding my empire. *But I'm only focused on the ones I'm building (and maintaining) today.*

Plus, I only focus on developing one or two new income streams per year, regardless of how many ideas I have. And, oh goodness, do I have ideas. I bet you do, too.

I have an annual strategic planning session at the end of the third quarter every year (coincidentally well-timed to coincide with my birthday). I *look* at my options, *choose* my income streams for the next year, and then *move* (take action).

Here's how you can use *look, choose, and move* in your strategic planning:

Look. Pitting one income stream against another with the criteria I've shared will yield a clear favorite or two, and this is where strategic planning comes into play.

Choose. You'll want to develop just one or two streams at a time over a year, and based on the criteria I shared above, you want to choose which one (or two) to work on for the foreseeable future.

Want ten income streams? Give yourself five to ten years to put this empire in place. Yes, ten years from now, you can have five, six, or seven-figure income streams (totaling multiple six, seven, or even eight-figures).

Put in the effort, and something you build tomorrow can pay for your trip to France in a decade.

Move. Once you've identified what you want to build, it's time to create a plan and get into action.

You'll recognize this process from page 12. It can really help you pick the right income stream(s) now and in the future.

Here's part of my process in the form of an example:

Example: Book + Journal + Course

Based on my book production schedule (both the list of books I want to write, and the production schedule for said book), I do the following:

1. Write an outline for the book.

2. Use the outline to create a landing page for the course, then put the course up for pre-sale in beta.

3. Write the first draft of the book, and send it to the editor.

4. Create course (record videos, craft collateral materials, refine course landing page, beg Lucas Marino to help me).

5. Review manuscript edits, and send to the proofreader.

6. Finish course materials.

7. Review proofreader's marks, and send the final draft to formatter.

8. Create a journal based on the final manuscript draft, have it proofed, and send it for formatting.

9. Launch the book and journal on the same day with the final version of the course.

Those nine steps are a high-level overview of the thousands of actual steps, but you get the point. Each business asset has its own production and publication or release schedule, yet while one is "at rest," I can work on another. In less than six months, I've created two new book products and one new course product.

Bonus: The pre-sales of the course fund the production of the book!

As you can see, you can intentionally create a new income stream with a very high level of success with proper perspective and planning. I hope you're excited!

Before the book is finished, however, there are other insights I want to be sure to share with you. Head on into the last chapter and take a look when you're ready.

CONCLUSION

INSIGHTS, FINAL THOUGHTS, AND BEST WISHES

Sometimes, I read a book, and what's presented is all sunshine and rainbows. I'm here to tell you that while I love being an empire-building entrepreneur, there are some days that are better than others.

It's impossible to build an empire without frustration, making mistakes, and sometimes feeling like you're wasting time and money. You may even have days when you feel like going back to having a regular job would be just fine, thank you very much!

In this book about monetizing your book, I've shared with you the potential upside of each income stream and set what I think are reasonable expectations. There are some additional thoughts I want to share with you, so you are infinitely prepared for what's to come.

THE REALITY OF EMPIRE-BUILDING AND BUILDING YOUR EMPIRE

"Framing reality" is the phrase Lucas used when I was describing this section to him.

Most experts only share the upside or best-case scenario, hesitant to tell the truth about the under-belly, what could go wrong, or how much time, money, or energy it could actually take to build an income stream and your empire. Also known as *the reality of monetizing your book and building your empire.*

The truth is that there are aspects of empire-building that aren't sexy or pretty. It bears repeating: Every income stream will most likely take longer, require more money and time than you initially think, and require more effort than you initially think.

That's great, though, because if you knew then what you know now, about almost anything in your life, would you have written the book, gotten married, or started the business?

In a word, *no*. Probably not, anyway. You'd have analyzed it from all angles and said, *"Hard pass! I'm not up for that!"*

But that's also good news, right? Wearing rose-colored glasses is sometimes the only thing that allows us to take risks, to fling ourselves headlong into the abyss, with a prayer in our hearts and five bucks in our pockets.

It can be tricky to balance maximum positivity with the reality of handling day-to-day challenges. Still, if I didn't mention how necessary this is, I would be doing you a disservice. If I made building an empire all kittens and cupcakes, you'd most likely be mad at me for not inserting some reality or, worse, turn your lack of "instant empire success" into a failing on your part.

Here are some quick insights into how to handle important aspects of income stream building, so you can have a foot in reality while you've got the other one on the next step toward massive success:

Match your activity to your goals. It's easy to say you have a goal or desired outcome. The not-so-easy part is making sure your activity is commensurate with your desire. For example,

I know several authors who *love* ideating around new income streams and even relish putting everything in place. However, they get defensive and shut down when marketing and sales are mentioned.

The path to achieving a goal is littered with milestones and targets. I know that to engage one new member of my mastermind, I'll need to have conversations with two or three individuals for whom it would be a perfect fit. (Incidentally, that number was much higher in earlier years. The longer you do something, the easier it gets.)

To write a fifteen or fifty-thousand-word book, I need to write every day, putting an average of one thousand words up on the board every day. I don't feel like writing every day, yet it's my job and I do it. There are several aspects of monetizing your book you won't feel like doing (anytime or every time). You'll have to come to terms with the unsexy parts of being an entrepreneur.

When you're not getting the desired results, analyze your activity to ensure there is congruency between what you want and what you're doing to get what you want.

Stay in front of the money. If you've ever had surgery and missed taking pain medicine, you've been behind the pain. You want to stay in front of your pain, just as you want to be in front of your money. Said another way, it's operating your income streams (and your business) as though you haven't yet been paid (even when you have). Being behind the money is being paid before delivering products or services, spending that money, and then losing interest in fulfilling your obligations.

I've seen service providers on a high from selling services, only to fail to provide stellar customer service. It's perfectly fine to collect all of your money upfront, but be sure to put yourself in the shoes of your client or customer and provide the best service you can—as if they haven't paid you yet. Trust me when

I say your name, brand, and reputation depend on it. You won't ever want someone to say, "I paid him, and he was fine for a while, but I'm underwhelmed with what was delivered."

Scared money don't make money. This is a phrase I first heard a dozen years ago, and intuitively, it made sense to me. It has since become popularized in a song of the same name by Young Jeezy.

Think of *scared money* this way: *The fear of taking action will result in inaction, and the fear that money you invest won't come back will result in exactly that—no money coming back.*

It represents the difference between a scarcity mindset: *There's never enough money* and *money is hard to come by,* and an abundance mindset: *There's always more than enough money,* and *money flows easily to me.*

If you want to monetize your book, it is imperative you adopt an abundance mindset. I mentioned *Prosperity for Writers*, but that book is just the start of your mindset work if you have any limiting beliefs around money. I've shared some recommended reading in this book's bonuses: HonoreeCorder.com/monetize.

Monetizing your book, building an empire, and entrepreneurship in general all have one thing in common: Revenue is rarely as consistent as the money earned from having a regular job. There will be times when you're flush with cash, and there will be times when you're wondering where it all went. And it could take *years* for you to have enough in reserve to weather those ups and downs with a mere shrug of the shoulders.

If being on the entrepreneur rollercoaster is uncomfortable to the point of anxiety (small or overwhelming), you have work to do. You must get comfortable with being uncomfortable. There will be ebbs and flows, that's a fact. If this freaks you out, you will want to embark on the consistent personal development required to overcome this anxiety and be able to lean into the ride. The best time to start working on yourself is today.

Under promise. Another very easy aspect of income stream building is to, in one's excitement, overpromise. You want the client. You can feel they're ready to say yes, and before you know it, you're offering to give them the equivalent of your bedroom while you sleep on the couch. Be clear about what you offer and aim to provide stellar service while promising to give less than what you can deliver. It will surprise and delight your client when you exceed the expectations you've set by a mile rather than promising what you hope you can deliver and missing the mark.

Work smarter, not harder. Working smart means you do the things that are solely in your area of genius. My superpowers are writing, content creation, strategy, and business development.

I'm not a graphic designer, accountant, attorney, or ConvertKit expert, so I have folks I rely on to handle the things I don't excel at so I can do only the things that move me toward my goals. I have a half-dozen members on my team (all independent contractors) who perform tasks and create assets I need for my businesses so I can work solely in my areas of genius.

You might think you'll save money and time by doing it all yourself, but what could take you three hours to figure out might take someone else five minutes. Give yourself the gift of folks who make your life and business run like a top.

Working smart also means you schedule time off every day, week, month, and year *in advance*. It also means you take time for yourself, family, friends, and hobbies. In addition to marketing your books and turning your expertise into other income streams (without a doubt, this is so much fun!), you'll need to find time for people and things that are not work-related. Your business will be all the better for it!

Fall in love with marketing, sales, and selling. You absolutely must understand *sales* and *selling* and *marketing* are a large part of your job. So, you might as well love it! Here are some suggested books to help you shift your perspective, if needed, to get the best results in the shortest period of time possible:

- Read *The Miracle Morning for Salespeople.* This will achieve several goals at once. It will help you make the most of your mornings by engaging in the practices of the most successful people on Earth. And this will ensure you are maximizing your days, as well as have an approach to selling that is relationship-based, effective, and fun.

- Read *Psycho-Cybernetics* by Maxwell Maltz. Understanding how your brain works and how to program yourself for success will allow you to do anything. This includes marketing and sales, and you'll do them on autopilot *because* you've created the mental pictures of your desired end results and the actions needed to achieve them.

- Read *Sell It Like Serhant* and *Big Money Energy* by Ryan Serhant.

- Not a book, but a solid tip: Get in the best shape and health of your life. When you feel fit and fantastic, you carry yourself very effectively, making yourself a magnet. The books I've recommended can also help you do that, in a way that feels pretty easy and incredible.

BE PATIENT.

Patience is a virtue for a darned good reason—it isn't easy to be patient! But to put income stream after income stream in place, patience is a key ingredient.

- **You'll need to be patient with yourself.** There's a steep learning curve, and you need to give yourself grace when it takes longer than you'd like to get the hang of something.

- **You'll need to be patient with others.** Yes, I know you want signed agreements, royalties, and large direct deposits *yesterday*, but your timing and your clients and customers' timing aren't always the same. And yes, I know you want partnerships that are easy, lucrative, and fun, but everything isn't magical all the time.
- **You'll need to be patient with how much time everything takes.** Just because something hasn't already happened doesn't mean it won't. *It will.* Give it time and be patient.
- **Read those paragraphs again.**

REST, BUT DON'T QUIT.

It's okay to take a break, get your bearings, and analyze why something isn't working yet. Take a break, eat a snack, call your coach, **but do not quit.** It is okay to rest, but I don't think it's ever okay to quit.

Your future self will thank you for sticking with it. Just yesterday, I was at a luncheon, and one of the attendees, an attorney, shared a quick story. He had a client who had unsuccessfully been trying to sell their company for quite a while. They'd created some software code they felt would benefit someone, but several deals had fallen through. The two main guys decided they'd just go ahead and make it open source, but their attorney (the guy telling the story) said, "Let me make a few more calls." Within a week, they'd sold their company for **$100 million dollars.** Now, you can't live on that, but it's a good start!😊

All of that to say two things: (1) you probably won't sell anything for $100 million dollars, but you never know! (And if you do, based on something you read in this book, I'm so excited. Also, I'm registered at Mercedes Benz USA.) (2) You just might be one more conversation, meeting, or email away from success, so please rest, but do not quit. Okay? Okay . . .

However, when you're tempted to quit, read *Three Feet from Gold* by Napoleon Hill and *The Power of One More* by Ed Mylett.

You can do this.

Successful people are no different from people who are not successful, with one exception. They had an idea, made a plan, and stuck with it until they were successful. (They did not quit.)

You can be successful. I promise.

If I, with barely a high school education, could write books and create new income streams every year, so can you.

I hope this book has inspired you to see your book as the source of endless possibilities and you monetize it one income stream at a time. And when you do, I hope you'll reach out and tell me all about it. I cannot wait to celebrate with you!

AUTHOR'S NOTES

Thank you for reading this book! When I wrote the book, I was excited to put the finishing touches on *The You Must Book Business Series*, and since **Building a Million Dollar Book Business** is my second most popular course, I knew getting this book out into the world could be very helpful to its readers.

Writing about each of the income streams I've developed through the years allowed reflection time and put me in an elevated state of gratitude. I've worked on incredible projects with amazing people and gotten to experience so much that I would have otherwise missed out on.

Because I have a high tolerance for uncertainty and low anxiety when it comes to the ebbs and flows of realizing revenue, I have taken a lot of risks—and many of them have paid off. Some of them have been painful failures. I'm just as grateful for them because I long ago adopted the belief that I either win or I learn.

There are some income streams I'm still working on that didn't make this book, and many other ideas that will pop up in the future.

But I'm most excited about the ideas you'll have because you've read this book. Won't you please send me an email and tell me which stream you're most excited about, and of course, stay in touch and keep me posted on how you're doing?

I hope you've enjoyed reading this book, it's stoked the flames of your desire to build multiple income streams, and our paths will cross in the future.

Honorée Corder

October 2023

GRATITUDE

Byron, you already know how much I adore you. Thank you!

To my mom, I love you.

Renee, thank you for being just the best. I adore you!

Jizelle and Tim, where have you been all my life? IFLY!

To the team that made this book possible, I appreciate you more than words can say! Karen, you're my friend and editor, in that order. You're the best, cookie! Jen, I love having you on my book production team. Amazing! Dino and Robert—your design work is next-level! Thanks, as always, for everything!

COURSES

Be sure to get the companion course to this book:
Building a Million Dollar Book Business
and multiply your income streams in an easy, lucrative, fast, and fun way!

Visit https://honoreecorder.com/bmdbb/ for more information, and use code **READER** for a special discount!

Get a complete book publishing, marketing, and monetization education with these courses.
Visit HonoreeCorder.com/Courses

WHO IS HONORÉE CORDER?

Honorée Corder is a prolific author with more than fifty books (including *You Must Write a Book* and *Write Your First Nonfiction Book*) with over four and a half million sold worldwide. She's an empire builder with more than a dozen six- and seven-figure income streams and the host of the Empire Builders Mastermind, plus she's a TEDx speaker. Honorée passionately mentors aspiring empire builders, coaching them to write, publish and monetize their books, create a platform, and develop multiple streams of income. Find out more at HonoreeCorder.com.

Honorée Enterprises Publishing, LLC

Honoree@HonoreeCorder.com

HonoreeCorder.com

https://www.linkedin.com/in/honoree/

Twitter: @honoree

Instagram: @empirebuilderusa

Facebook: https://www.facebook.com/Honoree

Printed in Great Britain
by Amazon

89343947-477b-4bca-b6fa-d94c25533362R01